PRAISE FOR AUTHOR BILL FROMM
AND *THE 10 COMMANDMENTS OF BUSINESS AND HOW TO BREAK THEM*

"BILLY FROMM IS A SELF-PROCLAIMED RENEGADE. William Fromm is a pragmatist. The combination of the two in *The 10 Commandments of Business* provides an insightful and entertaining look at the oxymoron called conventional business wisdom."
> — Alfred G. Goldstein,
> President, Sears Specialty
> Merchandising Group

"THIS BOOK COMBINES WIT, WONDERFUL STORIES, AND A LOT OF GOOD COMMONSENSE IDEAS that made reading it both enjoyable and thought-provoking."
> — Henry W. Bloch, Chairman and CEO,
> H&R Block, Inc.

"A REFRESHING ATTITUDE-ADJUSTMENT BOOK, which I describe as frolicking Fromm's business bible for transforming lonesome leaders into hugging heroes."
> — Paul Bishop, President,
> Young Presidents' Organization

THE 10

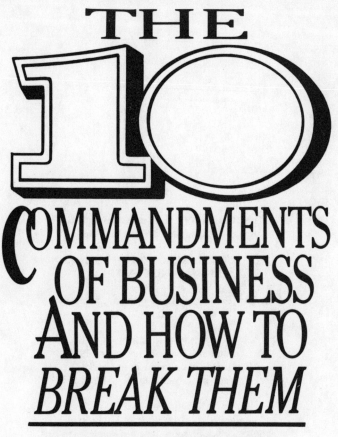

COMMANDMENTS OF BUSINESS AND HOW TO *BREAK THEM*

Secrets for Improving Morale, Enhancing
Customer Service, Increasing Company Profits,
While Having More Fun Than You Ever
Thought You Could Have at Work

BILL FROMM

BERKLEY BOOKS, NEW YORK

This Berkley book contains the complete
text of the original hardcover edition.

THE 10 COMMANDMENTS OF BUSINESS
AND HOW TO BREAK THEM

A Berkley Book / published by arrangement with
the author

PRINTING HISTORY
G. P. Putnam's Sons edition / April 1991
Published simultaneously in Canada
Berkley trade paperback edition / March 1992

ISBN: 0-425-13216-1

A BERKLEY BOOK ® TM 757,375
Berkley Books are published by The Berkley Publishing Group,
200 Madison Avenue, New York, New York 10016.
The name "BERKLEY" and the "B" logo
are trademarks belonging to Berkley Publishing Corporation.

PRINTED IN THE UNITED STATES OF AMERICA

10 9 8 7 6 5 4 3 2 1

ACKNOWLEDGMENTS

I AM AN AVID BOOK READER. I've read thousands of books, and therefore thousands of "acknowledgments." They all seemed pretty boilerplate to me until I had to write one of my own. I have now come to realize the incredible number of people, other than the author, that it takes to make a book happen.

Almost five years ago, Pat Curran encouraged me to take my unusual message around the country on the Young Presidents' Organization circuit, and he wrote letters to event chairmen touting my seminars.

Charles Mallory, my first editor, became my personal shrink. He constantly assured me that I had a book in my head that people would read. Had he not introduced me to Adrienne Ingrum at Putnam, this manuscript might still be in the third drawer of my desk.

Adrienne Ingrum was my first editor at Putnam. She kept after me to make the book as good as I could make it. When Adrienne left Putnam to join Longmeadow, Chris Pepe took over where Adrienne left off and educated me to the details of book publishing. My agents, Arthur and Richard Pine, have been a constant source of helpful ideas.

I'd need another volume to name all of the clients of Barkley & Evergreen and my coworkers, without whom the very ideas for this book would not exist. So let it suffice to say that I am deeply grateful to all of them.

A special thanks goes to Peter Gerstberger, CEO of The Berwick Group, Inc., in Boston, for graciously allowing me to incorporate their Basis of Competition cards into this book.

One of the unexpected joys of this experience was working with my son Andrew and with Laurie Bomba. Words cannot convey how proud I am of the contribution they both made to this book, and the joy that I had in working with them almost every day. It is a simple fact that, had they not been able to capture my speaking style and personality on paper, this book would not be what it is.

I'd also like to thank my other sons, Jeff and Daniel, for their input and encouragement; and my stepson, Kristen, for wondering if this book would make me famous.

I'd like to thank my parents, Martin and Dorothy Fromm, for caring about me so much. And finally, I thank my wife, Mickey, for teaching me to care about others.

TABLET OF CONTENTS

INTRODUCTION

SOME PEOPLE CALL ME A RENEGADE.

If "renegade" means that I often ignore the obvious answers in order to find the unique solution to a problem, I plead guilty. In this book, I have identified ten theories of business (I call them Ten Commandments) that are generally accepted but shouldn't be. Many executives would call them conventional wisdom.

But I have found that conventional wisdom in business usually proves to be a lot more conventional than it is wise. So, instead of trying to give you new ways to follow these rules, my advice to you is to break them. This book is full of alternatives to these conventional approaches—alternatives that have worked for me and my clients. Some of them may seem far out. But, if you stop to think about them, they make a lot of sense.

I don't suggest that you try and implement all of my ideas. Some of them probably aren't right for you or your business right now. Pick and choose those that your gut tells you will work best for you in your business and career. Trying to use all of my ideas, without considering whether they're consistent with your personality or business, will only make you end up looking like a poor imitation of Bill Fromm. Since my wife often reminds me that the original ain't all that great, use my ideas as a launching point for doing things your way.

Why am I out to undermine some of the most accepted views in business today? Because they don't work anymore. The most popular business practices have been around for so long that they're deeply embedded in our culture. No one ever sits back and asks what these rules are there for. They're etched so firmly in our minds that we don't see a need to reconsider why we're following them.

It's time to think again.

9

There is only one way to make a mark in business. And, it's not by following the rules. It's by breaking them.

TEGWAR

Years ago, I was a camp counselor. Right after we indoctrinated the first year campers with a few mild practical jokes, we'd help them part with some of their camp store money with a little card game called TEGWAR. TEGWAR is an acronym for The Easy Game Without Any Rules. The game calls for any number of players and at least one sucker. Every time the sucker thinks he's going to win a hand, he is informed that the rules for that particular situation are different. For example, kings are higher than queens unless you're the third person to lay down a card and you have brown hair. Of course, if I have brown hair, my king will win because my last name begins with an "F." It's a little more subtle than that, but you get the idea.

Managing people is like playing TEGWAR. In order to out-manage the competition, you've got to break the conventional rules and make up your own.

YOU CAN'T SHOOT POOL WITH A SCARED STICK

There's another game that I used to play as a kid that has managed to provide some relevant lessons for business: pool. If you've ever been in a pool hall playing for more money than you've got on you, you know that you can't shoot pool with a scared stick. Pool is an exact game. One flinch, and you've missed the shot. I don't care how high the stakes are; you can't allow yourself to be afraid of losing if you want to win. Confidence is the first ingredient that you need to be a great pool player.

My business philosophy is the same: no guts; no glory. Some people go to work and try to shoot pool with a scared stick. They're more afraid of losing than they are motivated to win. They allow their fear of looking bad to interfere with their business decisions.

When you work in constant fear of failure, you're destined to censor out some of your best ideas.

No one strives for mediocrity. But an awful lot of people settle for it. Managers who are mediocre are not mediocre because they're stupid or because they don't have interesting personalities. They're mediocre because they're more afraid of striking out than they are excited about hitting home runs.

This is not a book about getting lucky. I'm conservative when it comes to making business decisions. But if you want to be a home run hitter, you can't be afraid to seize opportunities when they're thrown your way.

In addition to being confident, a great pool player sees more shots than anyone else. Being able to see more opportunities for shots comes partly from experience, but it also comes from being able to be open-minded enough to see the opportunities that others don't see. Business is full of hidden opportunities.

One of the most unique people I have ever worked with is our company's chief operating officer, Ron Dickson. He's an unpretentious workaholic from Iowa with old-fashioned ideas and a catalog of one-liners that would rival Will Rogers's. In the years that I've worked with Ron, he has never come to me with a problem. He only brings me "opportunities." Problems are opportunities to Ron for two reasons. First, Ron really believes that problems present unique opportunities in their solutions. And second, solving a problem is Ron's opportunity to earn his keep. In his mind, that's what he's paid for, and if there weren't any problems, no one would need him.

How does one go about finding opportunities? You can start by questioning those business practices that you take for granted. You don't have to be a genius to open your eyes.

MARKETING GENIUS IS AN OXYMORON

One day while I was waiting to give a speech, a friend of mine introduced me with the following line, "I'd like to introduce a true marketing genius, Bill Fromm." I didn't know what to think. Marketing genius is like military intelligence—an oxymoron. Marketing strategy is not rocket science. It's good old-fashioned common sense.

The secret to successfully marketing any product or service is understanding what the customer really wants and then filling his need or desire. The secret to successfully managing people is to understand what they really want out of their careers and then to give it to them. The common tendency in management is to concentrate on what the manager wants from his employees. What he should be doing is concentrating on what his employees want from him.

Managing people to perform at a high level of quality and productivity isn't complicated either. The same emotions and feelings which drive people in their personal lives are also the motivating forces in their business lives.

When employees get what they want from their careers, their morale goes up. When employee morale goes up, product quality and customer service go up. When employee morale goes up, employee turnover goes down. All these factors help move profits up. There is a direct cause-and-effect relationship between employee morale and profits. For some reason, a lot of companies over the past 50 years felt that focusing on improving employee morale and customer service was a cost that negatively affected their bottom line. The fact of the matter is that increasing these two is a quick way to increase corporate earnings. In this book, you're going to find lots of ways to improve employee morale that will increase the quality of customer service and the company profits at the same time.

But you're also going to find lots of ideas that will raise your eyebrows and cause you to think I'm not playing with a full deck. Well, I've got news for you. Renegades do play with a full deck. They just don't play by the rules.

THY CUSTOMER IS KING

ONE OF THE FIRST things we learn in business is that the customer is king. I remember the first job I ever had. I was sixteen years old and the place was Peed's Flower Shop. My job was to come in after school and sweep up. It was usually busy, so I was also responsible for assuring impatient customers that someone would be with them in a minute. No matter how irate or pushy the customer was, I had to smile and be polite. That's because Mrs. Peed took me aside on my first day and explained to me that, in Peed's Flower Shop, the customer is always right.

You probably got a similar indoctrination at your first job. Almost everyone does. It's a good focus for people on the front lines to have.

But the rules change when you become a manager. For managers—be they chief executive officers of Fortune 500 companies or managers of small departments—THE CUSTOMER IS NOT KING. If you want your people to deliver outstanding customer service, then you need to treat them as if they were more important than the customers. The problem is that no one sits us down to explain this new philosophy when we first become managers.

The customer is not king? This is a threat to the very foundation of American business. Famous ad slogans, like "Have it your way at Burger King" and "We treat you right" at Dairy Queen, have always preached the supremacy of the customer. If the customer doesn't feel like a king, won't he run to the competition?

Absolutely. That's why you have to treat your people like royalty. How you treat your people will determine whether or not they treat the customer like a king.

Imagine that you are manager of a restaurant, and you have the world's best customer. This customer eats in your restaurant three times a day, 365 days a year. You can't have a better customer than that. On the other hand, you also have the world's best hostess. This hostess gets to work on time every day, and she's never sick. She can keep track of a restaurant full of people without missing a beat. What's more, she always has a smile on her face and she can remember every regular customer by name. You are managing a restaurant that has the world's best customer AND the world's best hostess. Tonight, one of them has to go. You pick!

Whenever I ask this question at my seminars, managers of all kinds vote to save the hostess. You see, the bottom line is that good hostesses are a lot harder to find than good customers. In fact, if you have a world-class hostess, you'll be able to find more customers. As a restaurant manager, I want my hostess to treat the customer like a king. But, I'm going to make sure that my world-class hostess knows that I think she's more important to me than any customer. That's how I'll ensure great customer service. And, that's how I'll keep my world-class hostess.

Customers are critical to any business's success. But, if you're a manager, you must make that transition in your thinking which places your people's interests ahead of all others. *Tell* your employees that the customer is king, but *show* them that they're royalty as far as you're concerned.

If you want to improve customer service, improve the way you treat your people. As their feeling of importance increases, the way they treat the customer will improve correspondingly.

Here's another way to think about it. A company can't possibly be the preferred service provider if it isn't the preferred employer. In other words, you'll find the best customer service at a company that's known for being a great place to work. Think about a company or store that provides great customer service. I guarantee they're a preferred employer in the industry. For example, ask any aspiring flight attendant where he hopes to work someday.

Chances are, his answer will be American or Delta. And guess which airlines consistently provide the best service? Furthermore, when employees (and former employees) of Eastern and TWA are driving around with bumper stickers that say "No Lorenzo" and "Dump Icahn," chances are the service isn't so hot at those airlines.

Great managers understand that in order to improve customer service, they have to improve employee morale. That's the real secret to making the customer king.

HAVE YOU FIRED A CUSTOMER LATELY?

Sometimes, you have to go to great extremes to show your employees that they're more important than customers. It may seem ludicrous to fire a profitable customer, but there are times when you can't afford not to.

Several years ago, I had a customer who was nasty. In fact, he was the nastiest person I've dealt with in 25 years of business. My lawyer suggested that I use his name. However, I happen to know that my lawyer and his wife are thinking about putting an addition on their home, and I'm not interested in having it called the "Fromm wing." So, we'll call this client Max. If you've been in the work force for very long, you've undoubtedly met someone who you think would put Max to shame. Everyone thinks their worst customers are worse than anybody else's.

It didn't matter what we did for Max; it was never right. It didn't matter how fast the service was; it was never fast enough. What's even worse, Max was rude and belligerent to our people. He cussed at them and called them words Eddie Murphy would be embarrassed to use. Once, he even threw a layout back at one of our art directors. Get the picture?

On the other hand—and there always is—Max's company did a lot of business with us. And they paid their bills on time, which counts for a lot in my book. But, nobody wanted to work on his account. The people who did work on it hated coming to work in the morning. I had a real dilemma.

One day, after another of Max's tirades against my staff, I called him up and told him I needed to come over to his office to talk. I didn't tell anybody in my organization what I was up to. When I got to Max's office, I told him that we were resigning his business, effective that minute. I assured him that we would expeditiously complete any jobs in progress, but we would take on no new assignments and we were looking to terminate the relationship as quickly as possible.

Max was flabbergasted. Nobody had ever told him to take his business and shove it. He had no idea that WE were unhappy with HIM. In fact, to my total amazement, he told me that he was very happy with our work. (Don't ask me how he treats people that he's *not* happy with.) In any event, I told him that as important as his business was to us, the mental well-being of our people was much more important. I explained to him that under no circumstance was our company going to do business with him. Then I left.

On the drive back to the office, I felt good. I'd stuck to my guns in placing employee service above customer service.

Back at the office, I immediately called a meeting of our entire staff. When everyone had assembled, I announced that we had just resigned Max's account. The applause, screaming, and whistling were deafening. It was like someone had just pulled the plug out of a huge emotional dam.

The outpouring went on for a few minutes; then I asked for quiet. I told everyone that before they got carried away in this state of euphoria, it was important to remember some of the earthly details that could very well affect their personal income.

I explained that we had just resigned a very significant piece of business that would affect bonuses at the end of the year. Nevertheless, I challenged them to work harder and smarter than they ever had so that the loss of business would be minimized. Nobody seemed to care much about the loss of business. They felt that they were going to have more fun at work.

As you might have guessed, everyone in the organization pulled together. An extra effort to attract new business was successful. By the end of the year, we had more than replaced the revenue that we had lost. As a matter of fact, we had the best year in the history of the company. And morale had never been higher.

If you let a customer unfairly abuse just one of your people, everyone in the organization is affected. The reason is that you're sending everyone a message that the customer can do anything he wants. You're telling your people that they're really not that important, and if it comes to a showdown, they'll be the ones who'll bite the bullet. When they get that message loud and clear, it will affect the way they treat all of your customers—even the good ones.

I don't advocate going out and firing a customer every time you want to give the troops an emotional boost. It can be a very expensive employee morale program. On the other hand, if your goal is to experience success as a manager over a long period of time, you have to occasionally make value judgments as to who is more important—the customer or your people.

To build a successful organization, everyone has to contribute. Sometimes you have to fire an employee who isn't pulling his weight. Customers make a different kind of contribution to your company: they pay the bills. But, customers are not exempt from being fired. Any customer who abuses your people will ultimately cost you much more than they can ever contribute to your profits.

- If you want the customer to be treated like a king, you have to treat the people you manage like royalty.

Thy Goal Shalt Be to Make a Profit

THIS IS A BOOK on business, so let's get right down to business and talk about profits. That's the bottom line, isn't it? You don't have to be a graduate of Harvard Business School to know that the goal of business is to make a profit. If you want to survive in a competitive marketplace, you've got to concentrate on making money. Sounds painfully obvious, right?

Wrong. The goal of business is not to make a profit. Even if the only reason you work is to get filthy rich, the goal of your business cannot be to make profits. Not if you ever hope to make any. You see, making profits is like making babies. Let me explain.

Back in the days when I was in the business of making babies, it was a relatively unexplored field. When a couple had trouble conceiving, there wasn't a lot you could do. A couple could see a doctor, but the best he could do was check to see that both partners were fertile. Remember, this was before the era of test tube babies and artificial insemination. So the couple would receive this advice: "Don't try so hard. Just let nature run its course." That advice was easier to give than to follow. If you really want children, you try hard. After the couple had spent several months attempting every quack method in the book, they adopted a child. You know the rest of the story: a month after the new baby arrived, nature kicked in and the woman became pregnant.

I see the same phenomenon in business. The principle goal of most companies is to make profits. Not surprisingly, most companies fall short. You see, making a profit is like making a baby. The best way to be successful at it is to stop focusing on it. Profits cannot be the goal of a successful business. Profits are the result of operating a successful business.

One problem with making profits the goal is that the long-term strategic health of the company is often sacrificed for short-term results. An increase in profits makes the financial health of the company look good right now. But a company can look good financially today and be strategically weak for the future.

A common mistake that people make, especially when their company is in a bind, is to sacrifice the strategic health for the financial health. That is to say that they will do anything to show a profit today, without caring about what happens tomorrow. Here are a few examples of how a focus on profits is shortsighted and can hurt a company in the long run.

A CEO at a public company wants to show a profit to shareholders every quarter. So he may end up with a dangerous, 90-day mentality. For example, he might ax the advertising budget one quarter because he's worried about profits. Sure, that quarter's profits will look a little rosier. But, what happens to the company's brand awareness when it drops out of the public eye? Competitors who didn't cut their advertising will have an easier time making inroads.

There are lots of ways that a manufacturing company could turn a quick profit. They could decrease the amount of goods they have in inventory. They could cut back on a shift at the factory while depleting that inventory. The immediate profit picture could look bright. But, their dealers won't be happy when the orders aren't being filled on time. And how will the customers react if they have to wait for the product because it's "on order" from the factory?

On a smaller scale, a restaurant manager might want to show a quick increase in profits to impress the owner. What are his options? He could decrease food costs or labor costs. For example, he could start cutting down the size of portions. Maybe he'll use fewer pecans in his pecan pancakes or buy lower quality produce. He'll make some money in the short term, but you can bet that the customers will notice.

If the manager cut back on the number of cooks, servers, or busboys, labor costs would go down and profits would increase. Temporarily. Once customers experienced poorer service, they'd find another restaurant to patronize.

Another problem with having profits as your goal is that most of your people aren't that interested in net profits before taxes, return on net assets, and all the other financial measurements that senior management worships. "Increasing profits" isn't a good goal to use to motivate your people. It isn't something that most people can rally around. In fact, profits won't motivate most people to do what you really want them to do.

Like 105
trophy
or good 105
When your focus is on profits, you lose sight of the business that you're in. Concentrate on running a good business, rather than making profits. The profits will follow.

I walked into a restaurant one day, and hanging on the entryway wall was a plaque that said that this was the most profitable restaurant in the chain. I felt like turning around and walking out. Obviously, their focus was on profits instead of great food or great service.

If you really need a quick fix that won't sacrifice the strategic health of your company, focus on improving employee morale. In most businesses, that's the fastest way to increase profits. Your employees are the ones who are responsible for delivering the product or service. If you can increase employee morale, productivity will go up, employee turnover will go down, and profits will increase.

The best way to improve morale is to make work fun. People want to have fun and take pride in their work. If they do, they'll work hard, and they'll work well. And, most importantly, they'll stick with you.

It's hard to motivate employees by concentrating on increasing profits, but you can increase profits by concentrating on your employees. So, stop worrying about making profits and start making work fun. In other words, forget about making babies, and concentrate on the sex.

WHAT ARE YOU WORKING FOR?

If you aren't working for profits, then what? Take a careful look at your business or department. What is it that you're trying to accomplish? If the only goal you can think of is to make money, you've got a serious problem.

If you manage a retail operation, maybe your goal is to try to build the most knowledgeable sales staff in the industry. If you're in the restaurant business, you may want to provide the healthiest food, the fastest service, or the most elegant dining experience. If you're a manufacturer, quality might be your goal. Whatever you decide on as the single most important aim of your business is your goal. For example, Avis wanted to provide the best service in the rental car industry, so they adopted "We try harder" as their goal and slogan. Federal Express is another example. They want to provide the most reliable overnight delivery service in the world. Hence, their goal and slogan: "When it absolutely, positively has to be there overnight."

Goals cannot be set by edict. If the people in the organization don't buy into the goal, you're doomed to failure. For example, if an airline set "on-time arrivals" as their goal, the pilots better be with the program. After all, they have a tremendous impact on punctuality, and they also get paid by the hour.

Before we go any further, let's clarify the distinction between "goals" and "objectives." I use "goal" to describe the banner that your company will march behind. Goals are infinite in time. They are not quantifiable. Goals are ideals that you can never fully achieve. They are something that people can rally behind, like the quest for the Holy Grail. In general, goals should be stated in less than ten words. Everyone in a company should know the goal, word for word. Not because they had to memorize it, but because it makes so much sense.

Objectives relate to the goal and support it. They are concrete, finite, and quantifiable. Objectives are measurable. Each objective must be achieved in a set amount of time. And when the time is up, there will be no question as to whether you've achieved it. It will be as easy as comparing a couple of numbers.

When Donald Peterson became president of Ford Motor Company, he set out to improve the quality of their cars. He established quality as Ford's goal. Quality was "Job One." This was a goal that everyone in the company could understand. Everyone wants to be associated with quality and take pride in his or her work.

Peterson supported his goal with objectives. For example, an objective might have been to decrease the number of engine defects by four percent by the new year. Mechanics who assembled those engines knew that the object was not to produce as many as possible, but rather to build them right the first time.

I'm sure Peterson was interested in increasing profits. The employees involved in Ford's profit-sharing program were probably interested, too. Nonetheless, Peterson's goal was not to increase profits. Profits were the result of achieving his objectives. In a time when the American automotive industry was being scoffed at for shoddy workmanship, Peterson put Ford back on the map.

If you're a retailer, your goal might be to provide the best service. With service as your goal, your objectives would focus on improving the customer's experience in your store. Measuring those types of objectives is as easy as "mystery shopping" in your store.

"Mystery shopping" is when researchers, playing the role of customers, go into stores to see if they are properly stocked with merchandise, if they are clean, and if the employees are properly trained and helpful. Mystery shoppers act like regular customers and buy merchandise. They keep precise tabs on how quickly store personnel respond to their being in the store, how long they wait in line, quality of service, appearance of merchandise, and so on.

Mystery shopping is a way to find out exactly how your company is doing from an objective viewpoint. It reflects how customers experience your business right now.

Not only can you use it to see if you're achieving your objectives, but you can also use it to get an idea of the strategic health of your company. You see, if your customers are happy when they leave your store, they'll probably be back. And, after all, repeat business is the most profitable kind.

I actually use mystery shopping scores to forecast my clients' sales. If the scores are going up, increased sales will almost always follow. If, on the other hand, the mystery shopping scores are declining, trouble is probably just around the corner.

The one thing that mystery shoppers shouldn't rate is individuals. They're not there to tell management who was naughty and who was nice. But they will tell you if they had a nice time at your store.

You don't have to own a big chain to benefit from mystery shopping. And you certainly don't have to hire a firm to do your mystery shopping. But you can't do it yourself, because your employees would recognize you. Instead, you can have a consultant, supplier, or even a friend do it for you. Develop your own standards with a point value for each category. If you set the perfect score to be 100, your objective might be to get an 80 in every category.

Be frank with your employees. Tell them that someone will be visiting the store to mystery shop. Explain the whole process. But most importantly, remember to tell them that this is not a time for them to be judged. You're not trying to catch individuals loafing. You're trying to get the customer's view of how your company looks.

If you're not the president of a company or aren't involved in setting your company's goal and objectives, you're still not off the hook. What about your department's goal? Or, for that matter, what about your own personal goal? The principles are the same. For example, your personal goal shouldn't be focused on your next promotion. Instead of concentrating on improving your position, concentrate on improving yourself. You don't get ahead by focusing on your next salary increase.

Several years ago I decided that my goal was to make work more fun for me and those I work with.

MISSION IMPOSSIBLE

A lot of companies use the term "mission statement" in place of "goal." In case you're unfamiliar with mission statements, they're highfalutin verbiage that is supposed to describe what a company wants to be when it grows up. But I have yet to hear a mission statement that wasn't too long. In fact, some of them run a full page or more. They're usually written with the intention of motivating employees, but I've rarely met an employee who can ever remember his company's mission statement.

Do you know what the mission statement is at your company? Unless you wrote it, you probably don't even know whether you've got one. If your company does have a mission statement, try this experiment. Find out how many people know what it is. If they don't even know what it is, there's not much chance that it's motivating them.

If you haven't figured it out by now, I don't like the term "mission statement." It's a nebulous, bureaucratic term. I prefer four letter words—like "goal." If you want to motivate your employees, don't come up with a mission statement. And if you've already got one, lose it.

KEEP YOUR EYE ON THE PIE

Many people believe that financial statements will disclose how well their company is competing in the marketplace. It simply isn't true.

The only accurate measurement of how successfully a company is competing in the marketplace is the trend line of its *share of market*. No other measurement will tell you. And, sadly, most companies don't know what their market share is.

In the late 1960s and early 1970s, my company, Barkley & Evergreen, did some work for a company that was in the business of making replacement mufflers and tail pipes. It was a sizable company, with double-digit sales increases. They were making a lot of money and thought they were doing great. I thought they were doing terribly. They were looking at their profits and sales increases, and they were happy with what they saw. I was looking at the trend line of their share of market, and I was worried because at the same time that they were making more money than they'd ever made before, they were losing their piece of the pie.

The reason is that during the mid-1960s, automobile manufacturers started making cars with dual exhaust systems. By the time those cars came into the replacement market, there were two mufflers and two tail pipes to replace, rather than one. The marketplace virtually doubled overnight. Even though the company had a significant sales increase each year, it was actually losing business to the competition.

I couldn't convince them that they had a problem, so we parted ways. They didn't notice the problem until their sales started to decrease, which was too late. Now they have a fraction of the sales they used to have and correspondingly low profits.

Consider how you measure the success of your business. Are you making the same mistake? Operating statements describe past profits or losses. They are historical documents and only tell you how a company has done in the past. They won't give you any clue as to the future. If they did, banks wouldn't make bad loans. Operating statements ignore the strategic health of the company—which more accurately predicts how it's going to do in the future.

The problem is that most CEOs spend more time looking at financial numbers than they do at marketing numbers. They have a tendency to hold financial statements very close to their hearts. And while the people at that tail pipe company were drooling over their financial statements, their competitors were taking away their market share.

Traditional measurements of success ignore how the competition is doing. The measurements don't take into account what's going on in the industry. They assume that your company exists in a vacuum. The fact of the matter is that your company exists in the marketplace. Your monthly sales figures mean very little unless you view them in relation to the rest of the industry.

The only measurement that takes into account how you're doing in relation to your competitors is the trend line of your share of market. No other measurement will tell you.

Profits won't tell you. You can make money while you lose customers to the competition. Just cut back on the quality of the goods or services that you provide while maintaining the price. You'll lose your repeat business, but you'll make huge profits until the customers run out. A company can gain a lot of money simply by harvesting—but it could be in bad shape for the future.

Return on net assets won't tell you, because that figure only reveals how the investors are making out. It doesn't consider the return that the competition is getting, and it won't give you any idea how the company is going to do in the future. You might as well consult an astrologer.

If I told you that a company had a 25-percent increase in sales last year, would that be good or bad? If the industry's sales were flat, that would be good; if the industry's sales increased by 40 percent, it wouldn't be good. What if that company's market share was seven percent one year and only two percent the following year? It's safe to say that they're in trouble. A trend of your share of market not only describes how well you are competing in the marketplace, it's also a good indicator of your strategic health.

To find out how your company is competing in the marketplace, you have to follow the trend line of your share of market.

SHARE OF MARKET MATHEMATICS

A lot of people tell me that they have no way to figure their share of market. They complain that large, sophisticated companies have all kinds of methods to find it, but smaller businesses can't afford these methods. When I tell people how to find their share of market, I simply point out two things.

First, unless you're in a big, high-stakes industry like network television, where one-tenth of a rating point equals millions of dollars, you don't have to know your share of market down to the zillionth decimal. All you have to do is be consistent in your method of measurement.

Second, a lot of research is available that you've already paid for. You continue to pay for it every April 15 when you pay your taxes. It's information from the government. And it can be very helpful in figuring your share of market.

During one of my seminars, a home builder remarked that he had absolutely no way to find his share of market. I asked him to define his market—all homes in a specific price range in the city, all homes of any price range in a certain portion of the city, etc. He told me that his market was all homes in a particular area.

I asked him if he needed to get a building permit when he built a home. Of course he did. Then I asked if other builders needed permits, too. Yes, obviously. So I suggested he get the number of building permits issued to home builders in the specific ZIP codes of his interest. Then he could divide that into the number of homes he built and have his share of market.

If you manage a grocery store, you'll find your share of market at the library. Find out how much the average family spends on groceries each month, and multiply that by the number of families in your trading area. Divide that number into your monthly sales figure, and you've got your share of market.

Is it exact? No. But it should give you a pretty good idea of how you're competing in the marketplace.

You don't have to spend a fortune in research to find your share of market. You just need to be consistent in how you go about it from year to year. Your share of market can be off by a few percentage points, because it's the trend of that share that's important.

You can reconstruct the data from prior years using company information. For most types of business, information on industry trends is as near as the public library. If it isn't there, try trade magazines and directories. And don't forget that big bunch of research you've already paid for through the government—the census.

Once you know your trend line of share of market, you can start to do your level best to send the trend upward.

- Making profits is like making babies: don't try so hard.
- Only share of market tells you if you're eating the competition's lunch.

RANK HATH ITS PRIVILEGES

IF YOU'VE EVER BEEN in the military, you know that R.H.I.P. is an acronym for Rank Has Its Privileges. That means that officers enter doors first, get into cars last, and get to the front of the mess line, among other things. The military has a pecking order, and it seems to work—for the military. But a private in the army can't decide to quit his job and go to work for another army because he doesn't like his commanding officer. A colonel doesn't have to worry that his sergeant will walk in one day and give two weeks' notice because a competitor made him a better offer.

A manager *does* have to worry about those possibilities. Nonetheless, most people in business are firm believers in R.H.I.P. They think that the higher they are on the organizational chart, the more perks they should receive, and the less dirty work they should have to do.

At the same time managers will tell you that rank should have its privileges, they'll also tell you that it's important to promote teamwork. Everyone wants teamwork. I've never heard anyone say that teamwork is bad.

When you separate "officers" from "enlisted men" in your organization, you end up with not one, but two, teams. And two teams don't work as one; they compete. It's a sure way to cause friction between management and employees. The one thing an organization doesn't need is an "us and them" attitude among the employees.

As a manager, too much R.H.I.P. can be fatal. One day, you

could turn around to make sure that everyone is following you and find that nobody's there.

R.H.I.P. should be replaced by what I call R.H.I.R.—Rank Has Its Responsibilities. And one of the primary responsibilities of a good manager is to work to flatten the organizational chart. The closer that you, as a manager, can get to the people you manage, the better chance you have that they'll be there for you when you really need them.

American car companies have always been really big on organizational charts and the perks that go with being "on top of the pyramid." In fact, American car companies have a lot more layers than their Japanese counterparts. That might just have something to do with the fact that U.S. car-makers are seeing their share of market evaporating.

With layer upon layer of management comes day after day of intrigue—sometimes called corporate politics. I've seen organizational conniving that would make most spy novels seem like kid's stuff. I've even seen "adults" make a big deal over who's chosen to sit to the left of the president at lunch. (Personally, I prefer someone who's left-handed.)

One way to eliminate unnecessary hierarchy is to destroy the ivory tower. Many offices are set up with all the "important" people clustered together. The example that immediately comes to my mind is the infamous fourteenth floor of the General Motors headquarters building. When managers are bunched together like that, they have nothing better to do than worry about what other managers are doing and who's scoring points with the big boss. A company doesn't need a "boss" department. Managers should have their offices near the people they manage.

One of my most successful clients is Western Auto. Terry Kuntz is their executive vice president of retail. If you're ever in Kansas City, you might want to go by Western Auto's headquarters and check out what floor Terry Kuntz's office is on. I'll give you a clue—you don't need an elevator to get there. Terry Kuntz is in touch with his people and his people are in touch with him.

Another method for dealing with the overcrowded conditions at the top of an organization is to turn the organizational chart upside down. In other words, your focus should switch from your superiors to the people you manage. If you believe that your focus is already on your people, put yourself to the test: do you spend more time worrying about how your boss thinks you're doing, or worrying about how your people think you're doing? Effective managers should be working for their people, not the other way around. When managers look down, instead of up, everyone gets taken care of.

When your goal is to help your people get their work done, a lot of the competition and petty jealousy will disappear. If managers at all levels of your organization have this same goal, you'll really have a team. And productivity will hit the ceiling.

WHO'S YOUR MVP?

Committing yourself to building a team is only half the battle. If you're trying to abolish R.H.I.P. in your organization or department, you also have to pull your people up. You have to be able to see beyond the hierarchy in order to appreciate the importance of everyone's job. A good start is to name your MVP.

At the end of a season, sports teams choose their "Most Valuable Player." In hockey, he's most often the player who scored the most goals or the goalie who had the most saves. In football, he's the star quarterback or running back.

Every company and organization should also have an MVP. I'm not suggesting that you single out one employee as being better than the rest. That would cause a lot of resentment. It would be like a parent admitting that he loved one child more than the rest.

The MVP in business has nothing to do with the individual merits of the person who bears the title. He isn't necessarily your star player. In fact, most MVPs hold jobs that would never be considered important by "traditional" standards. In fact, MVPs often occupy the lowest-payed positions in an organization. But they shouldn't.

Your MVP is simply the person who has the most direct contact with the greatest number of customers. Not the person who's responsible for the most revenue. Not the person who's in charge of the most people. Not even the person who works the hardest. He is the person who's responsible for the first impression on everyone who comes in contact with your company. Maybe in business, MVP should stand for "Most Valuable Position."

The MVP in our company is the switchboard operator/receptionist. This may come as a surprise to you, but I guarantee that it won't come as a surprise to anyone in our company. Every single person I work with knows that I believe our switchboard operator/receptionist has the most important job in the company. Nobody else in our company talks to every single customer, every single prospect, and every single supplier every time they call or come in.

How many times have you called a business and had the phone ring incessantly before it was answered? How many times have you been put on hold and wondered if anyone would ever come back on the line?

I don't like talking to a customer after he's been handled that way. In fact, I spend more of my time concerned with how we're handling incoming calls than I do any other single job in our company. That's because I want our firm to make a great first impression. Every time.

See if you can guess who the MVP would be in a restaurant? My vote goes to the hostess. She's the only person who sees every single guest who comes in, and she sees them first. She sets the tone. And if she is world-class, odds are that you'll be back even if the food wasn't quite up to par, or if the waiter was a little slow with the service. What's more, if she tells you good-bye on your way out, like she really hopes you'll come back, you probably will.

I want to have the best receptionist in the world, and in order to do that, we have to pay whatever it takes. If I owned a restaurant, I would pay whatever it took to have the best hostess in the world.

In a grocery store, the MVP would be the cashier. No customer leaves the store without seeing a cashier. You don't want to make your customers wait in a long line after they've decided to buy your products. If you can make customers happy with your product before they've even left the store, you're well on your way to having repeat customers.

In a hotel, the MVP is the doorman. I once met a world-class doorman named J.C. I don't even know his last name. That's all that was on his name badge: J.C. He was the doorman for the hotel that used to be called the Alameda Plaza (now the Ritz-Carlton in Kansas City). He was hired by Phil Pistilli, who was the president of the Alameda Plaza and a great recognizer of MVPs.

The first time I met J.C., I asked him what his initials stood for. He said, "Just Cash." The guy's got style. He's also got a great sense of humor and a quick wit. One time, he let me park my car at the front door while I ran inside to meet someone. When I came out, I wanted to give him a tip. But all I had was a five dollar bill, so I handed it to him and asked if he had change. Looking at the bill, he said, "That is change."

I always looked forward to seeing J.C. and joking with him. I would be disappointed when I went to the Alameda Plaza on his day off. I don't know what Phil Pistilli used to pay J.C., but I'm sure he was worth it.

Phil Pistilli was also president of the Raphael Hotels in Kansas City, Chicago, and San Francisco at the same time he ran the Alameda Plaza. To show you how consistent Phil's management style is, let me tell you about the doorman at the Raphael in Chicago.

I don't even know his initials, but I'll never forget his face. I was coming back to the hotel after dinner and, as I got out of the cab, I started to feel faint. Before I could take three steps, I passed out. (No, I hadn't been drinking—in fact, I rarely do.) The doorman caught me before I hit the pavement. He then carried me to my room and called the house doctor. He stayed with me and put cold washcloths on my forehead until the doctor arrived.

It turned out to be nothing serious. The next day, when I went to check out, I handed the doorman a $25 tip. He wouldn't accept it. He said that he loved when people tipped him to open a door, but he'd never accept a tip from someone in need.

Whenever I go to Chicago, I stay at the Raphael. The people I'm with usually think that I'm overly generous to the doorman. Little do they know.

Take a close look at your company or department. Try to find the person who is responsible for the customer's first impression. The person who occupies the critical point of contact with the customer is your MVP. Make sure he knows it. Make sure everyone in your company knows it. And, make sure that he is the very best you can find anywhere.

If you have an all-star as your MVP, it will go a long way toward making you look like a world-class manager.

DEAL EVERYBODY IN

Your MVP isn't the only unsung hero in your organization. All of your people should feel important. After all, if they're working for you, you must think they're good. Unfortunately, there are business traditions that, by their very nature, remind everyone that some people are more important than others.

In 1987, I abolished one of those traditions by starting one of the most successful employee morale programs we've ever had. It's quick to implement and has an immediate effect on everyone. The amazing thing is that it costs less than five dollars per person. I decided that every person in our company should have a business card. EVERY person.

In business worldwide, the way we identify the company we're with is by our business card. For some reason, we've let the distribution of business cards reflect the caste systems in our organizations. Why are business cards given to some employees and not to others? It's important for everyone in a company to feel important. We can't create a team when only some of our players have uniforms.

Does everyone in your company have a business card? A lot of managers would answer the question "of course not." And the two most common excuses I hear are these: first, most people in the company don't need business cards because they don't have anyone to give them to; and second, they cost too much money.

Nonsense.

If most people won't use many business cards, then it's obvious the cost of one year's supply will be negligible. If 25 business cards is a lifetime supply for the maintenance person, then it doesn't cost very much to keep him supplied forever.

If you deny business cards to the people who wouldn't be giving them away to customers and prospects, you are losing sight of the other reasons for providing them to your people. Someone who doesn't call on customers can still use business cards in a variety of ways. For example, if a friend or acquaintance asks where he works, he can give them one of his business cards with a sense of pride. If he's in a store, and a sales person needs to know how to reach him at work, he can whip out a business card.

When Western Auto hired our firm to help them develop a corporate culture program, only about 750 of the 8000 employees in the Retail Store Division had business cards. We made sure that all 8000 had business cards. One of the positive side effects of this decision is that when an employee gives a business card to a friend or acquaintance, they create additional awareness for Western Auto. Think about it. Wouldn't you rather shop where you know someone personally?

Here's a success story. A young woman just out of college came to work for us in a position that, in most advertising agencies, did not warrant a business card. Since everyone in our company is supplied with business cards, she had them. Her parents' next door neighbor was over for dinner shortly after she had joined our firm. He asked her what she was doing, so she proudly gave him one of her cards. Then, he asked her how she liked her job, and she went into an emotional monologue about how the company she worked for was the best in the world. She told him she was working harder than she ever thought she would and having more fun than she thought possible. When she finished extolling our virtues, he gave her his business card and asked her to pass it on to me so that I could give him a call. All of a sudden he was interested in doing business with our company.

I can think of a lot of more expensive ways to develop new business leads, but I can't think of any that are cheaper.

If you're not convinced that business cards can make a difference in the way an employee feels about his job, here's another story for you. In the summer of 1989, Barkley & Evergreen hired nine college interns. They worked full-time and did real work. We decided to give them business cards, complete with titles like "Student Copywriter" and "Student Account Executive." Interns with business cards? Am I nuts?

At the end of the summer, I asked each of them to write me a letter reviewing our intern program. When I waded through all of the pages of suggestions and compliments, I discovered that every letter had one thing in common. The best thing about the internship was the business cards. One student wrote, "Everybody told us that we were real employees, but the business cards proved it."

Those interns exchanged cards with each other. They sent them home to their friends and families. They gave them to clients. They pressed them in scrapbooks, portfolios, and diaries. We got more advertising mileage out of those cards than we would have gotten out of billboards. But, more importantly, the interns felt like real employees—and acted like it.

Summer interns who are just beginning their business careers aren't the only people who get excited about getting business cards. Most of the people in your company who don't presently have business cards will be getting them for the first time in their lives.

The cost of this program is so small and the benefits so great, you can't afford not to do it. When it comes to company pride, you don't want to be playing solitaire.

A LITTLE CARD TRICK

We at Barkley & Evergreen have another use for business cards. When someone gets a promotion, we take one of their business cards and, with a red pen, scratch out their old title and write in their new one. Then, we put the altered card in a small picture frame. At our next monthly staff meeting, we present the framed business card to the individual. And, of course, we reprint the business cards with their new title and give them a fresh supply.

If you go into the offices of most of our employees, you'll see the framed business cards on their desks or hanging on the wall. A few people take them home and put them on their mantles. In our culture, they're a sign that you've been recognized for an outstanding job.

While we're on the subject of employee recognition, there's something else we do to recognize new employees or to make special note of promotions. We send a news release, often with a picture, to the local newspaper announcing that the individual has joined our firm or has been promoted to a new position. Then, we take the article as it appeared, clip it out, and mount it inside a Lucite paperweight. It makes a nice gift for their desk or for an end table at home. These, like the framed business cards, are presented at monthly staff meetings.

Little touches like these cost less than a single sick day per employee. And when people feel appreciated and feel like they're part of a family, they do everything they can to show up every day. When someone's really sick, you don't want them coming to work. But, there are plenty of times when people are just feeling a little punk and have to decide whether to come in or stay at home. If they're treated right, the cards will be in your favor.

CULTURE BEGINS IN THE PARKING LOT

Business cards aren't the only traditions that create hierarchy in an organization. Other privileges of rank include assigned parking spaces, use of company cars or taxi vouchers, private dining rooms, use of sports tickets, and so on.

Some people argue that these kinds of perks are motivational. To them I ask, "For whom?" These privileges are incentive programs for the few. They're extraordinarily expensive because only a few people benefit from them.

Let me tell you a little story about a parking space. This was no ordinary space. It was the prime parking spot at my father's company. And, it was a convenient four feet from the office door. Fresh out of college, I went to work for my father. I'm an early riser and a workaholic, so I would get to the office well before most of the other people in the company. But, I didn't usually get there before my father; I inherited my work habits from him. When I pulled into the parking lot in the morning, his car would be parked in that prime spot. He was always the first one there.

But, if he was out of town, that prime space would stay empty all day. Why? Because it had a sign on it that read "Martin Fromm," and nobody—not even his son—would dare park in it. It would have been disrespectful.

Other officers in his company also had assigned parking spaces. The rest of the employees parked wherever they could find a spot. It didn't matter if you got to work early or late; you couldn't get a prime parking spot. They were reserved for the "important" folks.

When I started my own company, the first thing I did was negotiate a lease for our offices. When the landlord asked me how many reserved parking spaces I needed, I told him "only one." That one is for our employee of the month.

I don't have my own parking space today, and I never will. I usually get a pretty good spot, but it's not because I'm the president. It's because I get to work early. Whoever gets to work first gets the best parking spot. It's that simple.

I often hear executives complain that no one works as hard as they do and that no one comes to work as early.

That doesn't surprise me. If their people come in early, they have to park 50 yards from the building and walk by empty reserved parking spaces. That sends them a clear and concise message: "No matter how early you get to work, you're not as important as the people with reserved spots."

Parking spaces tell you quite a bit about the hierarchy of a company. The organizational chart of my father's company was painted on the parking lot. The closer a person's spot was to my father's, the more important that person was in the company. Every employee in the company knew whose space was next to my father's and whose space was farthest away, and it was no laughing matter.

When I call on a company, one of the first things I notice is whether or not they have assigned parking spaces for their executives. It tells me a lot more about their culture than reading a copy of their annual report.

YOU CAN TEACH AN OLD DAD NEW TRICKS

My father came to this country from Germany in 1933—one of many Jewish immigrants—without a dime to his name. In his new country, he was able to build his own business and prosper. He's a real Horatio Alger story. One time, when a local paper did a story about his success, he was quoted as saying, "I'll work full days until the day I die. Then I'll start working half days."

Through hard work, my father was successful—despite having assigned parking spaces. But when I showed him the manuscript for this book, he proudly told me that he intended to do away with his assigned parking spaces. Actually, what he said was, "What the hell. I get there first anyway."

Executive privileges should not be reserved for executives. Everyone likes getting a nice fringe benefit from the company. Even if it's only once in a while. At Barkley & Evergreen, we have a company van. We use it for deliveries and picking clients up at the airport. But on the weekends, anyone can use it. It's first come, first served, whether you're a vice president or an entry level employee. Some people use it to take the (extended) family to the ball game; others use it to haul their stuff around. People really appreciate it. And everyone benefits—not just a few.

WHO'S ON KP?

Sharing executive privileges with all of your people is just one of the responsibilities of rank. There are many more. And, they aren't all as painless as freeing up the good parking spaces. As a manager, you also have the responsibility to get your hands dirty.

Though it is your job to delegate, it is not your job to dump all of
the dirty work on your employees. There are some tasks that you're
better off doing yourself. I'm not talking about "important" stuff.
I'm talking about the menial tasks that aren't included in anyone's
job description. These jobs are different at every company, but an
example might be straightening up common areas or meeting
rooms between meetings.

Why should you be troubling yourself with those tasks? Because
they're boring and degrading. And if you delegate them, you're
saying that you're above it, and that your employees aren't. So stop
delegating the grunt work.

I did it because I had to. Employees at Barkley & Evergreen
weren't cleaning the kitchen and conference rooms when they were
done with them. And I wasn't innocent myself. My mother would
have been ashamed.

We have a cleaning service, but they don't wash out the coffee
pots, and they only come in at night. Like other companies, we
tried to clean up after ourselves during the day. But we didn't do a
very thorough job. Our conference rooms were used all day long,
and if there was an afternoon meeting, it was often the third or
fourth one in that room. By then, the place was a pigsty. It got to
the point where people were fighting over the 8:00 AM time slot.

After a meeting, the most senior person in the room would leave
and hope that the people left behind would clean up. Then the next
senior person would leave. You see, no one "important" wanted to
stay and help clean up because that would mean that they weren't
very important. People would keep leaving, one by one, until the
room was an empty mess.

Not anymore.

These days, when we finish a meeting in a conference room,
responsibility for straightening up, emptying the ashtrays, and
picking up any extra papers falls to the most SENIOR person in the
room. When I'm in a meeting, I'm responsible for cleaning up.

Funny thing: the minute I start to empty an ashtray or pick up an
empty Coke can, I have a lot of help from the other people who
were in the meeting. Without my saying a word, the room gets

cleaned up faster than you can imagine. In fact, I have to move fast if I'm going to have any chance of getting to a second Coke can before the whole room is clean.

As for the mess in the kitchen, cleanup is rotated weekly through all the departments. One week, it's the accounting department's responsibility to clean, and the next week it's the creative department's turn, and so on. However, the real responsibility for KP doesn't go to the department, but to the department head. With the department head in there working, it's amazing how fast the place gets cleaned.

I like to use the following scenario in my seminars to illustrate this point. Let's say that a restaurant is extremely busy and the manager is trying to turn the tables and seat the customers as quickly as possible. Let's also assume that a particular busboy isn't working as fast as the manager would like. There are two ways to handle this problem.

The manager can chastise the busboy to work faster. He may even threaten him with his job if he doesn't pick up the pace.

However, if the manager understands how to motivate people, he'll solve the problem by helping bus the tables himself. He'll go over to a table being cleaned and help the busboy without saying a word. He'll even clean faster than the busboy was cleaning. Guess what happens. The busboy picks up his own pace.

Successful managers aren't above any task. They realize that ivory towers can be wonderful places from which to watch the action, but they're terrible places from which to influence it.

As an aside, I advise you not to try this at home. A while back, I decided to put this new technique to work by volunteering to wash the dishes every night. I figured my sons would join in. Ten years later, they still haven't gotten the hint. Live and learn.

HAVE A HAND IN THE BUSINESS

As a manager, your responsibility only begins with the dirty work. You also have a responsibility to do everything you can to help your people get their jobs done.

Some managers are all talk and no action. They supervise and delegate and never venture too close to the actual work at hand. Good managers jump right in and help. Managers have to be willing to do whatever it takes to guarantee a perfect product and excellent service.

The next time you're eating in a particularly well-run restaurant, take a few minutes to watch what the manager is doing. You won't find him in an office leaning back in an executive chair. I guarantee you that he'll be helping the hostess with the guests that are coming and going, passing around the coffee, or helping the busboy clear tables.

Managers should view one of their primary responsibilities as helping their people get their work done efficiently. There's nothing wrong with doing some of their work for them. Your employees will appreciate the help and respect you for it. Meanwhile, you'll gain a better understanding of their jobs.

I can't leave this point without talking again about a man many consider to be one of the outstanding hotel executives in the country. Phil Pistilli started his career washing dishes at the Muehlbach Hotel in Kansas City in 1954. After college, he returned to the Muehlbach where he eventually became president. In 1968, he left to become president of the Alameda Plaza Hotel in Kansas City when it was just an architect's rendering. Until 1989, when the Alameda Plaza was sold to the Ritz-Carlton chain, Phil Pistilli served as president of what many people considered to be the finest hotel between Chicago and Los Angeles. Today, Phil and his son, Kevin, own the Raphael Hotels in Kansas City, San Francisco, and Chicago, and oversee the management of the Allis Plaza Hotel in Kansas City.

If you want to find Phil in one of his hotels, you'd better not be searching in the executive suite. Phil understands that his job is to make everyone else's job easier. To that end, you will probably find him behind the front desk during peak check-in and check-out times. And, when the coffee shop is at its busiest, Phil will be doing whatever the coffee shop manager needs done. That includes doing what he does best: washing dishes.

Phil Pistilli believes that the reason it's lonely at the top is that you don't have anybody working for you up there. You just have a whole lot of people for whom you work.

CUTTING RED TAPE

It goes without saying that a manager performs at his best when his people are performing at their best. With this in mind, it's surprising that so few managers actually work for their people. It's to your advantage to do everything in your power to help your people.

When I first decided to write this book, I began paying a lot more attention to different managers' definitions of their jobs. When I queried people who were presidents of organizations about their managerial duties, they described responsibilities to shareholders and reporting to the board of directors. And when I asked managers who were a little closer to the reality of getting work done, they talked a lot about hiring, training, and motivating the people who report to them. Nothing surprising. But one day I heard a speech that changed my perspective.

I was in Bermuda for a conference when I heard a speech by the president of McDonald's, Michael Quinlan. The subject of his talk was his company's approach to marketing, but it was his response to a question that interested me most. He said that one of the most important aspects of his job—and one at which he spent approximately one-third of his time—was cutting red tape.

The more I thought about it, the more logical it became. In any organization, most people are there to perform specific tasks. They don't have the authority or the time to plow through the bureaucratic malarkey. It is the responsibility of the manager to clear a path so that his people can do their jobs.

Think about the two-week period prior to any Super Bowl and you'll find a familiar scenario that goes something like this:

The media have all converged on the Super Bowl city and are looking for anyone who can give them even a shred of a story. They're interviewing assistant coaches, trainers, ball boys, vendors—anyone they can find. Then, someone pins down a head coach and asks him what he's trying to accomplish in the days prior to the game. He won't talk about the game plan or motivating his players. Invariably, he'll say that his primary responsibility is to deal with the media and other distractions so that his players can get on with preparing for the big game.

Authority is a tremendous resource. In your quest to help your people perform at their best, you have to clear them a path.

Any organization—no matter how small—is full of bureaucratic red tape. Policies, procedures, and chains of command can cause even an efficient employee to move like molasses in winter.

Even if an employee has a solid understanding of the procedures, he might not be as familiar with them as you are. If an employee needs to push something through the red tape fast, you ought to be there to take care of it. Nothing is as counterproductive as sending an employee back to the starting block because he's made a procedural error.

It is extremely difficult for a person who is low on the totem pole to sift through the red tape. In addition to being unfamiliar with the procedures, he has to move up the organization. And when he has to consult with a manager other than yourself, he'll undoubtedly be relegated to the bottom of that manager's priorities.

When your employees need to expedite a service or product, they need your help. You have the authority to move across the organization—instead of up it. If your people need to get something approved by a manager of another department, that manager will listen to you long before he'll listen to them. You can run right through the red tape.

You can also use your authority to eliminate red tape at your suppliers. If one of your people calls a supplier with a request, he'll deal with someone at a comparable level in that company. If he has an important request, you should place the call for him. You have the clout to get through to the boss.

As manager, not only are you more adept at moving through the red tape, but you're also more qualified to cut it. Perhaps you can authorize overtime at the last minute, so your people can finish a rush job. Or, you can approve an unexpected expenditure.

Let's say that you're a manager of a warehouse. Your policy is to ship via truck. One of your best customers across the country needs his order by tomorrow morning. In order to satisfy this customer, you decide that the items should be sent by Federal Express. You see, you have the authority to avoid some of the unnecessary steps in the procedure. If one of your people wanted to make that recommendation, it might take him a week to get approval.

Nowhere will you find a better example of red tape than in big government. I had the opportunity to spend a week with Gennady Gerasimov, who is the head of the information department in the Ministry of Foreign Affairs of the USSR. I was his host at a meeting in Acapulco at which he was a keynote speaker.

In the information department, Gennady Gerasimov manages approximately 120 people. Curious as to how such a high Soviet official views his management responsibility, I asked him what he did. He said that he had a "very big scissors" and used them "to cut red tape." This man has obviously figured out that in order to get his job done, he's got to clear a path for his people.

Red tape can sometimes come in a disguised form. When our telephone operator first started with our company, I noticed that every time I called the switchboard, my call was immediately answered—no matter how busy she was. I explained to her that my call was the least important one she received. After taking care of the incoming calls, everyone else's internal calls should take precedence over mine. I can wait for the people who do the work.

AVOIDING RED TAPE

Managers have a responsibility to help their employees get their work done. But they're not the only ones who have authority. Everyone has some amount of authority. If you are an aspiring manager, there's a lot you can do to get around that mountain of bureaucracy.

For example, let's say you'd like to put together a company softball team. If management takes a long time to give feedback on suggestions, or if it takes forever putting them into effect, you need to take action yourself. Don't run to your manager as soon as you have an idea, because, if he's not completely informed on the subject, he may raise objections, such as, "Stevensen tried to put together a team last year and it didn't work out."

You certainly have the authority to circulate information, or to post a sign-up sheet on the cafeteria bulletin board. Find out how much interest there is in your idea. The more organized and enthusiastic you are, the more likely people will want to get involved. Then investigate the local leagues and make a note of the cost and the time commitment. Be thorough, and be prepared to answer any and every question before you talk to management. Once you've covered all the bases, present your idea to your supervisor. You'll find management much more receptive to your suggestions after you've checked everything out. They'll be more confident sponsoring a team when they're sure that there is a lot of interest and that there aren't any hidden costs.

If the company won't foot the bill, don't give up. This is a chance to show your leadership skills. If you can get people enthusiastic enough to chip in for the registration fee and equipment, you'll have yourself a softball team.

Don't think that just because your supervisors didn't support you, they aren't going to appreciate what you've done. They'll certainly be impressed that you were willing to go the whole nine yards for your idea. And, you can be sure that they won't forget your ability to take charge when it comes time for your review.

A young man had been working at Barkley & Evergreen for just a few months when he organized a skydiving club. He discussed his idea with a few employees, found some interest, and went ahead with it. Now the skydiving club is the talk of the office. I was impressed. Not only did this man put together an exciting social activity entirely on his own, but he had the self-confidence to gather support for it after only a short time at the company.

If you're an aspiring manager, you may not find many opportunities for showing your leadership skills in your job description. In that case, you should keep your eyes open for opportunities. The next time you find yourself saying: "They should change the way they do that" or "What this office really needs is . . . ," take action. If you're lucky, your suggestion may be enough. But, if you really want to stand out as a leader, you'll be much better off taking charge of it yourself.

WHO'S IN CHARGE HERE ANYWAY?

Whether you're the manager of one or two people or the president of a large corporation, you have the opportunity to have control over the details of what goes on in your area. You have the power to ensure that even the littlest things are done exactly the way you would do them yourself. But, if you have any idea what it's like to work for a controlling manager, you won't exercise control; you'll give it away.

Marty Brown is one of the most unforgettable characters I've ever met. He's been a customer, coworker, adviser, and a second father to me for almost 25 years. He's owned more businesses than I can count. And he's the source of one of the best pieces of management philosophy that I've ever heard.

One day, I went to him for some advice on a decision. I had already spent many hours contemplating the pros and cons of this particular situation and I was stumped. When I explained my dilemma to Marty, he admonished me for not delegating the decision to someone else in the organization. He told me that I was exercising too much control and that I was meddling in the affairs of my employees. He went on to tell me that I was wasting my time.

He was right. Although at the time it seemed like a very important decision, now I can't even remember what it was.

He gave me this advice: as manager, you should only concern yourself with the crucial decisions, of which there are only a small handful per year. The rest of the decisions are minor and should be delegated to somebody else.

Here's Marty's reasoning. First, by letting others make most of the decisions, you free yourself up to spend more time with customers and employees. Second, when you let employees take part in the management of the company, they feel more comfortable with the decisions that are made and more responsible for the welfare of the company.

The problem is determining which of the decisions are major, and which are the ones that you should pass on to somebody else. Distinguishing between major and minor decisions is much like distinguishing between major and minor surgery. Major surgery is when you're under the knife and minor surgery is when it's somebody else. When it's your responsibility, it's easy to mistake minor decisions for major ones.

Put yourself to the test. For the next few days, keep track of every decision you make. Make a list and then sit down and review it. Review each decision and ask yourself whether or not it was really important for you to make it. If it wasn't, you should have had someone else make it.

Delegating decisions instead of tasks makes your job a little easier and your employees' jobs a lot more exciting. When you delegate tasks, you're putting horse blinders on your employees. Work is more fulfilling when people understand where the work is coming from and where it's going.

By letting others make decisions, you're encouraging them to take more responsibility for the work that they're doing. People are sure to want to do a better job when they can stake claims on the quality of the work that's produced.

There are some roadblocks to making this transition in your management style. And your desire to be in control isn't the only thing that gets in the way. Most people are used to having others make decisions for them. Almost every time a new manager starts reporting to me, I go through the same ordeal. Every day, he comes into my office with a question, "How do you want me to do this?"

It would be very easy for me to tell him. But every time, my answer is the same: "Well, how do you think we should do it?" The first time a new manager is in to see me, he usually responds quite lengthily. I reply: "Fine." Pretty soon, people realize that those decisions are theirs.

If you're president, there are many executive decisions that you can't delegate to just one person. Those should be delegated to the management committee. I'm not talking about your typical management committee. Almost every company has one. It usually consists of the senior executives in the firm. They make the "important" decisions in the company. Some of these management committee meetings remind me of a college fraternity meeting that I had the misfortune of attending. We had decided to have a party after finals were over. The emergency meeting was called for 8:00 P.M. on a Wednesday during Finals Week, just three days before the party. Nobody could agree on whether we should have french fries or baked potatoes with the steaks. No kidding. The meeting lasted an hour and a half. And the final decision was corn on the cob.

Management committees should not waste time pondering how to serve the spuds. My recommendation is that your management committee *not* consist of the senior management of the firm. Ask a senior management person (not the president) to chair the committee. Then draw the rest of the committee from the middle levels of the company. Put them to work making the bulk of the decisions.

Of course, there will still be a few major decisions that only you can make. One of my major decisions was to limit the amount of company dollars the management committee can commit. Any decision involving more than a certain amount of money has to come before an executive committee or the senior management person responsible for that area of the business. Otherwise, the management committee is free to make decisions—not simply recommendations that senior management can veto.

We have a year-end bonus pool in our company. The management committee decides the amount of the bonuses for everyone in the company except themselves and the senior officers. After all, who has a better handle on the people who are really getting the work done? Our management committee also deals with issues like summer hours, new employee orientation programs, and committee assignments for company events.

After you've started using this kind of management committee, you'll find some significant changes taking place in the attitudes of the people on the management committee, as well as the rest of the employees.

First of all, the people on the management committee will act more responsibly. When you give people the privilege of making important decisions, they usually act more responsibly.

Secondly, the rest of the employees in the company will feel like they are part of a team. After all, they're better represented in company decisions when their fate isn't decided by one person at the top of the hierarchy of management.

Most importantly, it makes leadership positions accessible to more people.

Whether you're a manager or a president, you have to be able to relinquish some control. It's not your job to make every decision. Figure out which are the decisions that have to be made by you. And let your people, or the management committee, decide the rest.

BACK TO THE FUTURE

There's another advantage to delegating decisions. The people who work for you represent a body of knowledge much greater than your own. That knowledge can be especially helpful in the area where the amount of information is most overwhelming: technology.

Let's face it. Technology is changing every minute. This year's science fiction movie could be next year's defense plan. And, business technology is moving just as fast. The information that your people have on this subject is invaluable to your organization. If a manager insists on maintaining control in this area, he could make some costly errors. Instead of making a hasty decision, or spending money on consultants, find out what your people have to offer.

For example, if yours is like most companies, you've got two groups of employees as they relate to computer technology.

On the one hand, there are the computer illiterates. These people could very well be some of your brightest employees and smoothest salespeople. The problem is that they may have finished school prior to the computer revolution. Although it's certainly possible for a young person to be computer illiterate, I think you'll find that the majority of this group will be over 40.

On the other hand, there are the "byteheads." You may discover that your most junior employees have the most sophisticated knowledge of computers. It has more to do with the classes they took in school and their interest in exploring than with their job responsibility.

These two basic groups present a significant problem and a stupendous opportunity.

Here's the problem. If your company is going to continue to grow through the next century, your people have to be prepared to deal with tomorrow's technology. As part of your company training program, you should offer some basic courses in computers. Maybe you can get one of your employees to teach it. If you're like a lot of managers I know, you may be well-advised to enroll in the course yourself. I'm 48 years old, and I'm just starting to get the hang of it. Another 48 years and I'll have it down.

The opportunity lies with the people in your company who have good computer skills. Remember, these may be some of your non-managers. Now you have a chance to give them a significant role in shaping the future of the company.

Here's what you do. Find out which of the people in your company are computer literate, and give them the responsibility for making decisions on technology at your company. You can find someone in management who is knowledgeable about computers and business technology, and have him chair a new committee. Call this new group the 2000 Committee. Any employee in the company can apply for membership. People will be selected to serve, not on the basis of their rank, but rather on the basis of their interest in future technology. This committee will meet every month to discuss how new technology can be applied to your business.

For example, if you're thinking about buying a new telephone system, give the responsibility for recommending a system to the 2000 Committee. When it's time to get a new copier, fax machine, desktop publishing system, or computer, your 2000 Committee will be the perfect group to analyze the options and make recommendations.

In addition to making better decisions, there's another benefit to having a 2000 Committee. People who, up until now, have had little or no role in shaping the future course of the company will have an opportunity to get involved. It will bring a new enthusiasm to their work and a new excitement to the whole company. It'll also go a long way toward flattening your organizational chart and making everyone feel more like a team.

So what are you waiting for? The year 2000 is not too far off. If you don't hurry up, you'll have to call it your 2100 Committee.

POWER TO THE PEOPLE

Moving from hierarchy to teamwork is no small change. You have to encourage employees to think and act independently. For most managers, that's not easy, and sometimes it involves changing a name or two.

In high school, I was a discipline problem. On those rare occasions when I wasn't getting into trouble, I was trying to weasel out of it. That all ended one day after school in 1958, when I was throwing snowballs at the school building. It just so happened that the vice principal, Gordon Wessner, watched me throw a snowball right through his office window. The window was closed at the time.

Mr. Wessner called me into his office. I could tell he was fed up. I was scared. In fact, I was so scared that I started making deals with God: "Dear God, get me out of this one, and I'll never hit my sister again." As if in answer to my prayers, Mr. Wessner offered me one last chance. He wouldn't throw me out of school if I'd turn over a new leaf. I jumped at his offer.

But Mr. Wessner's offer had a condition. I had to change my name from "Billy" to "Bill." You see, Mr. Wessner knew a thing or two about reforming "discipline problems." He knew that it would be easy for me to slip back into my old ways unless I were continually reminded of our deal. So, from that day forward, every time someone called me "Billy," I had to tell them to call me "Bill." My request called attention to the fact that a change had taken place. The new me was supposed to be more mature; hence, a more mature name. That was the last time I had to go to the vice principal's office.

I had forgotten about Gordon Wessner's philosophy until I began developing a corporate culture program for Western Auto.

Western Auto has 350 company-owned stores. Each store in the chain is set up as a separate profit center. Each acts as an individual business. All of the profits at Western Auto are made in those stores. So headquarters exists to serve them. Nonetheless, until recently, Western Auto had only one president. It's been a while since he's sold a set of tires. His office is at headquarters, where the only cash register is in the cafeteria. (They lose money in the cafeteria.)

The store managers deal directly with customers all the time. They have bottom-line responsibility. And, they make business decisions on their own. So, as part of their new culture program, and in honor of good old Gordon Wessner, we changed their names.

Today, Western Auto has hundreds of presidents. Every store manager now has the title of store president. And, all the assistant managers are now managers. These people were already presidents and managers at each store anyway—it was simply time to give them the appropriate titles. Imagine what it did for their self-esteem and sense of responsibility. And, when people at headquarters call, they're reminded that they're dealing with the most important people in the company.

To further ensure that the folks at headquarters realized they were working for the stores instead of the other way around, we produced new name badges. Now, when people from headquarters go out in the field to visit the stores, instead of wearing a badge that says "headquarters," they wear one that says "pit crew."

You see, Western Auto is in the auto parts and service business. We decided to use an analogy to auto racing. A race driver can't win without a great pit crew. They're the support critical to success. But, at the same time, a pit crew has to have a great car and driver. All the elements must work well together; but, the pit crew ultimately has to remember who they work for.

The effects of these changes are being felt right down to the customers. How does it sound when a customer comes in and asks for the manager, and the salesperson says, "Would you rather see the president?" And, if the president is unavailable, now there is always a manager in the store. Furthermore, since headquarters is consistently treating the store presidents and managers like the important people that they are, the customers are getting better service.

Obviously, everybody can't be a president. But, you should take a look at what your employees are doing for you. If they're doing presidential work, or if you'd like them to start, maybe it's time to give them the title. For example, there are lots of presidents in a hotel besides the person in the corner office. There's the head of housekeeping, the food and beverage manager, the sales manager, and the person in charge of maintenance. All of these people are presidents in their own right. Maybe they should be presidents in title as well.

- Rank has its responsibilities.
- Eliminate your caste system—you can't build teamwork from an ivory tower.
- A manager can avoid red ink by helping his people cut red tape.
- Empower people by moving decision-making down the organization.

THOU SHALT SCORN NEPOTISM

ALMOST ANY BOOK on management will tell you that business and family don't mix. When a company becomes nothing more than a family dynasty, the employees will feel resentment. Furthermore, hiring friends and family frequently backfires into an incurable case of office politics. Work is work. And home is home. And it should stay that way.

This commonly held sentiment causes managers to go to great lengths to resist a family atmosphere at work. Most managers believe that there should be different standards of behavior at the office than there are at home. Work is no place for affection; it's a place for formalities and personal distance. The workplace is no place for emotion—just the facts.

In keeping with this business practice, businesspeople speak in cold euphemisms. Charlie Sheen's character Bud Fox shows a mastery of this euphemistic language in *Wall Street*. His favorite parting remark was "talk at you." You can't get much colder than that. Bud Fox wasn't interested in conversation or communication—just in giving orders. He was equally tough when discussing his personal life at the office. When his colleague asks why he stopped dating a particular woman, Bud's cool response is, "She asked the wrong question: 'What are you thinking?' "

Bud Fox is a fictional character. But he demonstrates the way that people in business like to keep emotion out of their work. Emotion is reserved for home.

But the truth is that you can't shut off your emotion like a faucet when you get to the office. A formal business environment is cold and unnatural. Nonetheless, a cold atmosphere seems to pervade almost every workplace.

The traditional separation of "work" and "family" has become so complete that the words have taken on opposite meanings. People need to feel a sense of belonging at work.

THE ONLY GOOD BUSINESS IS A FAMILY BUSINESS

I'm not necessarily talking about mom and pop stores. Every company can benefit from a family atmosphere. It's your job as manager to create one. I've got some good news and some bad news on that subject. The good news is that a family atmosphere is most likely already hiding in your organization.

Most of us spend more waking hours with our business associates than we do with our families. Many people view their co-workers as family. In today's mobile society, fewer people than ever work in the same city where they grew up. Young people seek out cities where the job market is good. Entire families will change cities if the primary breadwinner is offered a better job. The era of the company town is long gone. People pack up and move just about anywhere for a good job. Consequently, they don't have a lot of family and childhood friends with whom to spend their free time. They don't have roots in the city where they work. It's only natural that the people they work with are important to them. They want the office to feel like home.

The bad news is that you can't spring this family atmosphere on people overnight. In fact, you can do a lot of damage to morale by rushing people into something they're not ready for. I've got a lot of suggestions for bringing out the family in your office. But they're suggestions, not prescriptions. Only you can know whether the people in your organization are ready for these changes. If they're not, take it slow.

As a manager, you are responsible for the financial and emotional well-being of the people who work for you. Whether you like it or not, people look up to you. It's your job to care about every success and do all you can to help them be the best that they can be.

You can't afford not to. When you're trying to meet a deadline, you need someone you can bank on. There's no one more dependable than family. People in a family work well together and feel a genuine responsibility to each other.

I took someone from my company with me to one of my seminars. During my talk, I mentioned that people in our company work an average of 50 hours a week, even though they're almost all salaried and aren't paid for overtime. One of the people in the seminar turned to my associate and asked her if we really put in those kind of hours. After she confirmed it, he asked why. She thought about it for a little while and replied, "Because if we didn't, we'd be letting our friends down."

People don't work for companies; they work at companies. People work for themselves and they work for their friends—their "family." They care a lot more about their friends than they care about corporate profits. If you can create a family environment, where the group's goal is to get the work done, productivity will noticeably improve.

So, aim for nepotism. Now I'm not suggesting that you put all of your family on the payroll. Nepotism, in its classic form, can be the ruination of a business. But, when you can instill a feeling of family among the people you work with, you will have the most powerful form of nepotism you can find—you will have nobody but family working for you. And you will have nothing but success.

A FAMILY THAT PLAYS TOGETHER STAYS TOGETHER

Many managers believe that nothing can be as destructive to employee morale as a good old-fashioned office romance. They think that it's just plain bad policy to allow it.

Trash that antiquated policy that says employees can't date each other. Where else do you expect them to meet people when they're spending most of their waking hours at work? Besides, all you're doing is encouraging people to sneak around the policy. You should encourage all kinds of after-hour activities among employees—be it golf on the weekends or ball games after work. Once strong personal relationships develop, they can be powerful assets when the going gets tough.

In highly successful companies, people don't forget the office when they leave the building.

I remember reading some comments by George Brett of the Kansas City Royals about his team's poor performance during the season following their 1985 World Series victory. He said that in looking back over the less successful year, it seemed that there weren't as many team parties at players' homes after the games. Brett said that the team hadn't felt as much like a family as it had the year they won the World Series.

Watch what happens when the workday is over to see if you're working at a place that has this sense of family. Do people go out for a drink or dinner together after work? If everyone goes their separate ways when the whistle blows, it's highly doubtful that there's a strong sense of family in the company.

GOLDEN PARACHUTES CAN LEAD TO A FREE FALL

Golden parachutes are a way for executives to bail out of a company and make a lot of money in the process. A group of senior executives in a corporation get together and arrange a package that allows them significant rewards when they leave the nest. You can hardly pick up a *Wall Street Journal* these days without hearing one of these stories. I wonder if the practice would be as acceptable if it were regarded as a parent jumping ship on his family.

Imagine the psychological and emotional impact on the rest of the people in the organization. They are, in effect, being told that they will be left to fend for themselves under new ownership. In this instance, senior management is obviously more concerned with their own future than they are about their employees. How dedicated do you think the employees will be after finding out about this?

Contrast this with two stories about my good friend Don Ross.

The first story took place in 1979. Don was president of one of the divisions of Dayco Corporation. The CEO of the parent company called Don into his office one day and told him about a new executive incentive program. Don was to receive a number of executive incentive units that could be converted into stock.

Don wouldn't have it. Instead, he requested that his allotment be divided among him and his people.

Several years later, after Don was promoted to president of Dayco, the company was sold. The new owners were anxious to retain Don and, to that end, wanted to quickly negotiate an attractive package for him. However, Don wasn't in such a hurry to feather his own nest that he forgot about the people who had helped make him indispensable. Before he would agree to negotiate his deal, he insisted that his people be taken care of first. Don took good care of the employees of Dayco Corporation. How dedicated do you think they were to Don Ross?

JUST LET ME BE YOUR TEDDY BEAR

Caring about the people who work for you is a crucial step toward developing a good family. But there's a big difference between caring about your people and caring about what they can produce for you. And believe me: people know which is which. In a business relationship, a manager cares that his employee is sick because the absence will cost him time and money. But, a manager like Don Ross has a family relationship with his employees; he's truly concerned about the well-being of his people.

The best managers demonstrate a caring attitude. How do I know this? I've done my own informal research on just this subject. I belong to an international organization called the Young Presidents Organization (YPO). More than 6500 CEOs from approximately 70 countries belong to this group. As a member for over 10 years, I've had the opportunity to get to know some of the most successful executives in the world. I've conducted management seminars for them and the senior executives of their firms.

Additionally, I've had the opportunity to work with all types of managers in companies with whom we've done business for over 25 years. It's been an incredible learning experience and has exposed me to more management styles than I thought possible.

The truly outstanding leaders come from a variety of backgrounds. Some possess advanced college degrees and some barely made it through high school. Some came from families with a great deal of money and others lived in poverty during their childhoods. These managers cut across every nationality, religion, and race. Some are men, and an ever-growing number are women. They come in all sizes and shapes—although I've noticed that the vast majority keep pretty trim.

When I think about these successful managers—who motivate others to achieve levels of performance far above the norms for their industries—I realize that there is only one common thread that ties them all together.

Great managers hug.

They have such a love for people, all kinds of people, that they can't keep their feelings inside. They show their feelings and they don't discriminate on the basis of rank or sex. They just hug. They hug their staff people. They hug clients and suppliers, too. The reason is simple: they're friends. A relationship with a supplier or client is like any other relationship. Either you grow together or you grow apart. Although some people may seldom show emotion, relationships aren't neutral. Think of anyone whom you come in contact with on a regular basis. If you've known him for a few years and you see him regularly, you have feelings for him. If those feelings are positive, it's a good idea to let that supplier or client know—with a hug. You can bet on one thing. If you have a customer that you hug, you probably have a customer that's going to stick with you.

In 1988, I attended a sales meeting of 200 managers of a large midwestern company. The company had experienced less than stellar performance for several years, and as a result, had just gone through a major executive reorganization. On hand to greet the group were a brand-new president and vice president/operations.

A banquet was held after the three-day series of meetings.

Certain individuals were recognized for their efforts over the past year, and everyone got a pep talk. At the end of the evening, the two new officers went to the ballroom exit to say good-bye to everyone as they left. Here's the clincher: instead of shaking hands, they both hugged every single person who left that room. This was their family that they were saying good-bye to. I actually saw some tears being wiped away. Would you like to guess what kind of year the company had? You guessed it.

You can't become a hugger just by hugging, though. I've seen people try, and it never works. A friend of mine who heard me give a speech about huggers decided he was going to hug everyone, too. The next morning, out of the clear blue sky, he started using a hug instead of a handshake. He literally went on a hugging craze.

It didn't work. It was superficial. He didn't really like hugging his people because, in many cases, he didn't really like them. He had surrounded himself with people who made him anxious, suspicious, and resentful.

That's not uncommon. We expect the office environment to be a little cold—definitely not affectionate. So that's what we create.

If you think that you'd like to make the change and become a hugger, you can't do it tomorrow. A major change like that takes time, for some people even a couple of years. It depends how entrenched you already are in your old way of doing things.

Hugging isn't a business technique. It can't be instantly overlaid onto your personality. If you don't feel it, you won't really be a hugger. Maybe you've put yourself in a position where you don't really love what you're doing or the people you're working with. That's an indication that it's time to change things so that you feel good enough to become a real hugger.

But there are some things that you can do right away that will make a difference. Start to show some affection at work. Even if it's just a friendly smile. Look at the people around you. Are they receptive to your gestures? Maybe the next time you have to hire someone, you should make sure that he's someone who is comfortable in a real family environment. It's the little things that you do that will bring on the bigger change. Remember, you can't become a great hugger right away. You have to work up to it.

When we hire a new employee, or get a new client, I don't start hugging them right away. That would be awkward. We build a relationship. It's no different from a friendship.

There are a lot of huggers out there who aren't hugging at the office. Maybe they feel it's not proper office etiquette or maybe they're worried about a sexual harassment suit. (If that's the case, use your judgment. There's a big difference between a friendly hug and harassment. You have to know what's appropriate.) If you're a hugger at home and socially, but not at the office, come out of your shell.

When you do, the first thing you'll notice is that you've probably surrounded yourself with a lot of other huggers. You see, huggers attract other huggers.

Hugging shows you understand and care. I can't begin to tell you how many times someone in my company comes to my office for encouragement. Maybe they're just having a bad day. What they get in addition to a pep talk is a hug. If you're going to be a successful manager, you've got to learn to hug. Not only that, you've got to mean it.

HAPPY HOLIDAYS

Families celebrate family events together. My most vivid early childhood memories are of my family during the holidays. Birthdays, anniversaries, and other holidays mean a lot to people. Everybody wants those days to be memorable.

Remember, I told you that most people consider their coworkers as part of their family. Well, there are family holidays at the office, too. Unfortunately, few managers recognize them. Either they're blind to the fact that these holidays exist, or they fail to realize how important they are to their people.

I've got a little experiment for you. Some day, when you've got a minute or two, ask ten people in your office a question. Either ask the first ten people you see, or hunt around for a good cross section of your firm. You can ask them individually or, for dramatic effect, round them up and ask them as a group. Tell them that if they don't know the answer immediately, they should NOT guess. Here's the question: "What is the month, day, and year you started working here?" Would you believe that nine or ten out of ten know the answer?

I've done this same exercise with more than 5,000 employees of different companies all over the United States. Well over 90 percent answered immediately. This almost always comes as a shock to their managers. These people probably couldn't think of their wedding anniversaries that fast, or their children's birthdays, or even their children's ages.

If the date people started to work for your company is so important to them that they can instantly recite it, what are you doing about it?

The answer I most often hear is "nothing." Some companies honor employees in the month of their anniversary. I don't think your spouse would appreciate it if you honored your wedding anniversary on some arbitrary day of the month. You don't get any credit for getting the month right. You'd be better off forgetting it altogether.

I know that most companies honor employees on their "major" anniversaries like the fifth, tenth, and so on. But that means that the date passes with the employee remembering it and the company ignoring it four out of every five years.

The irony of skipping the first four anniversaries is that those are the most important ones. After someone has made it five years, the most difficult times are already behind them. The first four years are the difficult ones; that's when people need the most encouragement. Imagine how unmotivating it is to have those anniversaries pass by unnoticed. It's like having your mother forget your birthday, or worse yet—ignore it.

One of the simplest, least expensive, and most effective ways to let your people know that they're appreciated is to recognize their employment anniversaries. Managers should write a personal letter to every employee on his anniversary. I know that sounds like a big job, but it's a lot easier than it seems, and well worth the effort.

All you need to do is get a list of all your employees' start dates from your personnel department. Write a short congratulatory note and think of something personal to say to each employee.

In addition, you should try to get the president of your company to write a similar letter to each of your people. If you don't know the president, try sending him a note asking that he send an anniversary letter to a certain employee. Tell him a little bit about the employee and how you think the congratulatory letter would be appreciated.

You may prefer to aim a little lower, but remember, the higher the person is in the organization, the more your employees will appreciate being recognized by him.

If you're the president and you have many employees, set up a system so that you can do a few letters each day. If you can't think of anything personal to say to an employee, talk to his supervisor. You may have to standardize certain portions of the letter. But it can still be personal.

John Barlow, president of Western Auto, will send out 8,000 anniversary letters this year. We designed a computer program, which was organized by anniversary date, name, and nickname. We used a merge program, and included paragraphs depending on the person's department. John personally signs 40 letters a day. He spends ten to fifteen minutes first thing in the morning. All it took was a little time and thought at the beginning. The cost of all of this: just fifty cents per year per employee.

If you don't have thousands of employees, you can write each and every letter. I do. Regardless of how many employees you have, sign every letter. And, mail it to their home. You can't believe the impact it will have. I have more people come up to me in our office and thank me for their anniversary letters than I have thank me for their bonuses—and we give hefty bonuses.

Most managers will never do this. They're too busy. It's not that important. The question I ask these people is this: "What better thing do you have to do?" There is no job that can't be delegated—except recognizing your people. YOU have to take the time to write a personal letter. People know you're busy. That's why it means so much to them when you take time to show them that you care.

I suggest that you go even further than just a letter, however. This is a special occasion. Why don't you find a small gift to show your appreciation? If you can't use company money, use your own. A coffee mug or a plant only costs a couple of dollars. Even a small gesture will be appreciated.

At Barkley & Evergreen, we have a company gift for every anniversary. Here's our gift list:

1st year:	sweater with company logo
2nd year:	jacket with company logo
3rd year:	attache with monogram
4th year:	set of 4 mugs with company logo
5th year:	four Waterford crystal wine goblets and wine
6th year:	rugby shirt with company logo
7th year:	cotton jersey cardigan with company logo
8th year:	sweatshirt and sweatpants with company logo
9th year:	plush terry cloth bathrobe with company logo
10th year:	six Waterford crystal cordial glasses and decanter
11th year:	wool crewneck sweater with company logo
12th year:	beach towel with company logo
13th year:	carry-on travel bag with monogram
14th year:	suitcase with monogram
15th year:	eight Waterford crystal champagne glasses and champagne

We try to give apparel as often as possible for two reasons: first, people like something that they can use; and, more importantly, Barkley & Evergreen clothing becomes a point of pride to the people in the company. It's like a merit badge in the Scouts. If you happen to be walking around in a Barkley & Evergreen crewneck sweater, people look up to you; you've been with the company eleven years.

I had a business meeting with a client at my office one day. It was 100 degrees and humid. A young woman walked by us in the parking lot. My client said, "Did you see that?" I replied, "I see her every day. She works for Barkley & Evergreen." He said, "No—she was wearing a wool sweater. Doesn't she know it's hot out?" I wasn't surprised because I had presented it to her the day before at our monthly staff meeting. Although I had sent her a letter congratulating her on the day of her anniversary, I presented her with the gift in front of everyone at the meeting. There was no way she'd come to work the next day without it.

Employee turnover is one of the greatest drags on profits. Reducing your rate of turnover will do more to increase your profits than almost anything else you can do. That's why you must recognize your employees when they stick with you. Every employee. Every year.

If over 90 percent of your employees can remember the day they started with the company, I would guess that 100 percent of them know their own birthdays. So, don't forget to send them a card.

If you've got a relatively small number of birthdays to keep track of, keep a file folder of cards and pick something suitable for each individual on your list. If you've got thousands of employees, you can have your own company birthday card designed each year.

We go beyond birthday cards in our company. We also give out birthday gifts. We select one item each year to be the birthday gift for everyone. One year it was a nice pen and pencil set. Another year, dinner for two at a fine restaurant. This year it's a $40.00 gift certificate good at any shop in Kansas City's world-famous Country Club Plaza. The point is that families celebrate big events together, and if you're going to be a family, you have to do the same.

When we take on a new advertising client, we immediately get started on our first two assignments—a birthday card for their employees and a birthday card for their customers. When you specially design a card for your customers that is unique to your own business, it demonstrates an attention to detail that everybody notices. Because many advertising agency clients like to change copy when it's first presented, last year's card for our clients said that we had finally developed some copy that was so appropriate that they couldn't improve on it: "Happy Birthday."

You can also have a lot of fun being creative with the birthday cards that you give to employees. For example, this year's card that we designed for Western Auto shows a group of people on a hydraulic car lift singing "Happy Birthday." Inside, the card says, "We thought we'd give you a little lift on your birthday."

Everybody likes to hear from family and friends on their birthday. Employees and customers are no exception. In case you wondered, mine is December 11.

Anniversaries and birthdays aren't the only special occasions that we recognize at Barkley & Evergreen. We'll use every opportunity we can find to have a family celebration.

Like Mother's Day. Despite what people think, men and women don't do an equal amount of work. At the office, they're both equally productive. But at home, some women have many more responsibilities. Even though times are changing, I'm sure they're not changing fast enough for many women. To show our appreciation for the people in our office that have two full-time jobs, we celebrate Mother's Day. We give a plant to every woman in the office.

And we just recently started a new tradition. In early December, the company rents out a Christmas tree farm for one day, and every employee gets a free tree. We encourage them to bring their families out and chop down the tree of their choice. It's usually a cold morning, so we all huddle around a fire, drink apple cider, and eat doughnuts. Just like family.

MANY HAPPY RETURNS

Another big part of treating your people like family is being able to forgive and forget. Every now and again, a former employee comes knocking at your door hoping to get his old job back. Whatever his reasons for quitting were, he's forgotten them and wants you to do the same.

People are sometimes surprised to hear that we make it a practice to rehire employees who have worked here and quit. Among those who have left our company and come back are two partners, two group supervisors, the head of training, and the vice president in charge of new business. In fact, the vice president is back for the THIRD time. What do you do when someone who voluntarily left your company a few years ago wants to return?

Let's assume he left on good terms with the company and with you. He wasn't fired. He didn't make any parting remarks that could be construed as bridge-burning. And when he worked there, he was well liked by his coworkers. In essence, we're talking about someone whom you didn't want to leave when he turned in his notice. He simply thought that he had a better opportunity to advance his career elsewhere. And now, for whatever reason, he's decided that the grass wasn't greener on the other side of the fence.

The biggest reason that you might advance for not taking him back is that you don't want the people in your organization to think that they can leave and come back any time they want. Half your company would take an extended vacation, right?

Forget it. Employees know that they don't leave a permanent void in a company when they quit. They can't count on finding an opening when they return. There's a sizable risk involved in that game.

Most companies won't take back an old employee, and they're missing a valuable opportunity. There are some tremendous advantages to having an open-minded view of rehiring people.

First, when someone comes back, he becomes a walking salesperson for your company. He's going to be telling other employees that your business is a lot better than many of the others they might be considering. He was out there, and he didn't like what he saw.

Second, the person who returns has just given you a terrific recruiting tool. After all, what better fact could you tell a perspective employee than that the people who leave your company are often sorry that they did and want to come back?

Third, former employees don't take as long to train as a new employee who's never worked there before. They can probably hit the ground running on their first day on the job.

Fourth, former employees offer few surprises. You already know their strengths and weaknesses.

Fifth, and most importantly, your people will recognize that you're somebody who can forgive and forget. You're compassionate. You treat the people who work with you like part of your family. And, even when your family moves out of the house or out of town, your feeling for them doesn't leave.

The ultimate compliment that a former employee can pay you is to tell you that he wants to come back and work for you again. If it happens, you know that you're doing something right in the way you're managing the business.

So don't automatically say no. It might just be that one of your best hires ever is a rehire.

DON'T FORGET YOUR EXTENDED FAMILY

If the people who work at your company are your family, then your suppliers are your extended family. You depend on them. You should take care to make sure they feel like part of the family.

Most managers take great pains to treat their customers well. And they should. But too many managers forget to show their suppliers a little appreciation and respect.

Suppliers are almost as important as your people. Naturally, you don't see them nearly as often as you see your employees, so they don't get the special treatment that your people get. But when suppliers do visit, you should treat them like you treat your own people.

And when it's a supplier's birthday, you should send him a card. If you know him well, you should recognize other special occasions, too, like Christmas or the birth of a new baby. I suggest that you give all of your people some company note paper and encourage them to write notes to the suppliers they deal with when occasions arise.

The fact of the matter is that most suppliers serve more than one client. There's a difference between a supplier who gives you service because he has to and one who gives you service because he wants to. If you happen to be the client who has the best relationship with a supplier, you can be sure that he'll be there for you when you need a special favor or a rush job. It's your job to ensure that your suppliers look forward to coming to your company—that they view every visit as a family reunion.

Managers don't get anything done by themselves. You depend on your people and suppliers if you hope to succeed. If you want to make certain that they produce, you can try two approaches. You can give orders to your servants and hope that everyone will heed your warnings. Or you can make requests of your friends and family. The first approach has been around since the invention of the whip. But it doesn't work in today's business world.

On the other hand, if you've got a strong and loyal family, you can't lose.

- Make nepotism a state of mind—treat everybody like family.
- Hugging isn't sexual harassment.
- Take a tip from Kodak: celebrate the moments of their lives.
- If you didn't fire 'em, rehire 'em.

THOU SHALT KNOW WHAT THOU SELLETH

REGARDLESS OF THE BUSINESS that you're in—whether you specialize in power drills, communication systems, or health insurance—you have to be an expert on what you're selling.

With that philosophy in mind, most companies work hard to ensure that they have a knowledgeable sales staff. When a customer inquires about a product, there should be a sales person on the scene to extol its virtues. A lot of companies orchestrate extensive training programs and instruct their sales staff on even the minutest details of their product or service. And, they should.

The problem is that most companies are so wrapped up in what they're selling that they give little thought to what the customer is actually buying.

Let me explain. One day, when I was flying from Los Angeles to Kansas City, a thought went through my mind. Instead of flying United, why wasn't I flying Santa Fe or Union Pacific airlines? After all, at the turn of the century, the railroads practically owned the transportation industry in this country.

The reason I wasn't flying Santa Fe was that the railroads never understood what business they were in. They thought they were selling transportation by train. But what the customers were buying was an efficient way to move people and cargo. If the railroads had really known what business they were in, they'd probably own the airlines today.

The landscape of American business is littered with companies that didn't know the business they were in. They focused on what they were trying to sell rather than what the customer was buying.

Toy trains are another example. When I was a kid, the toy I wanted most for Hanukkah was an electric train. Specifically, a Lionel train, which at that time was by far the major brand of electric train. Every kid I knew wanted a Lionel train set.

Since I got my Lionel train 35 years ago, things have changed. Lionel still makes trains. But most kids don't want to buy them. Lionel thought they were in the model train business instead of the toy business. And when kids wanted toys other than model trains, Lionel got left at the station.

You don't have to look back 35 years to see a toy company that didn't understand what the customer was buying. Several years ago, Tonka Toys introduced a new toy. Tonka Toys was already famous for making trucks. In fact, they sold a complete line of vehicles—trucks, cars, ambulances, etc. Their new toy was a vehicle that could be manipulated into a robot, and vise versa. Tonka was the first toy company to come up with this concept, so they could have named it anything they wanted. But since their culture was trucks, and because these new toys were vehicles that became robots, they decided to name them GoBots. GoBots were an overnight success.

When there's a new idea in the toy industry, whoever comes out with it first usually wins. That's because new toys are introduced at the annual toy show. This national exposition attracts toy buyers from all over the United States who place orders for the Christmas season. The Christmas season accounts for nearly 60 percent of annual toy sales. If you're the second one to introduce a toy, you literally have to wait a whole year—until the next buying season. With a one-year head start, you'd think GoBots had it made.

However, the following year, a similar type of toy was introduced by Hasbro. They could have named it anything other than GoBots. But before they decided on a name, the people at Hasbro spent some time finding out what kids were really buying when they asked for GoBots. They watched kids play with the toys. They discovered that kids liked the *process* of changing the vehicle into a robot. Kids weren't nearly as interested in the fact that it started out a vehicle and ended up a robot as they were in the process of changing it from one to the other.

This late entry was appropriately named Transformers. And its advertising focused on the process, which is what the kids were after. Hasbro focused on what the customer was buying. And they literally knocked GoBots off the shelf.

Figuring out what your customers are buying is very important. I spend a lot of time with my clients doing just that.

Once when I asked a man what business he was in, he said he was in printing. So I rephrased my question and asked him what his customers were buying. "Printing," he laughed.

I told him that our advertising agency works with many printers. So do our clients. But we don't want to buy printing; we want to buy attractive brochures, catalogs, and other pieces that are useful for our work. You see, we're not buying "printing." That's just the process.

I don't think of myself as being in the advertising business. That's what I say at cocktail parties because it's short and sweet. But that's not what we tell our clients. We're in the business of increasing their market share. No one wants to buy advertising. Companies wish they didn't have to advertise to get business. But they do want to increase their market share.

A good example of a company that knows what the customer is buying is IBM. If you've ever talked to an IBM salesman, you know what I'm talking about. The hardest thing to get an IBM salesman to do is talk about the hardware. Ask him about bytes and RAM and he wants to show you an example of an accounts receivable report or inventory control. Ask about memory and disk drives and he'll talk about their service policy. IBM understands that they're in the business of providing businesses with an accurate, quick, and economical method to manage information. IBM also understands that nobody wants to buy a computer; they want to buy what a computer will do.

Whether you're the owner of the company or one sales person on a staff of hundreds, understanding what the customer is buying is of tremendous importance. Now that I've given you plenty of examples, try to redefine your business by completing the following statement in terms of what your customer is buying:

We are in the business of _____.

Just remember, people don't want to buy drills—they want to make holes.

Who are your competitors?

Once you've succeeded in redefining the business you're in, you'll find that your competition has changed. Consider the following companies and try to guess who competes with whom:

1. Rolex
2. Timex
3. Volkswagen
4. Mercedes-Benz

Your first tendency might be to group them by the product that the company makes. But that's the wrong way to go about it. Your first step should be to define what the consumer is looking for when he considers each of these products.

1. Rolex—a status symbol that, by the way, tells the time.
2. Timex—a watch that is efficient, reliable, and economical.
3. Volkswagen—a car that is efficient, reliable, and economical.
4. Mercedes-Benz—a status symbol that, by the way, gets you where you want to go.

Only two of these products compete, and they are Rolex and Mercedes-Benz.

Either a person wants to buy a status symbol or he doesn't. If someone has a substantial amount of discretionary income, he may decide between a Rolex and a Mercedes. You're not going to sell that person a Volkswagen, because he's looking for a status symbol. Likewise, you're not going to sell someone a Rolex if he's "just looking for a watch."

Competitors aren't always easy to recognize because sometimes they don't sell the same product as you do.

Lee Derrough was in the audience at one of my seminars. He was then the president of Worlds of Fun, which is a subsidiary of Hunt Midwest Enterprises. I was discussing how to find competitors. Someone in the audience commented that he envied Lee because Worlds of Fun is the only amusement park in a 250-mile radius, and therefore has no competition.

Lee disagreed. He replied, "We're not in the amusement park business; we're in the entertainment business. We compete with movie theatres, the Kansas City Royals, the Kansas City Chiefs, the zoo, miniature golf, swimming pools, and golf courses." Lee competes with almost anybody who offers a good time.

Lee understands what business he's in, and he knows who his competitors are. That's one reason why he was promoted to president of Hunt Midwest Enterprises.

If you understand your product in terms of what the customer is buying instead of what you're trying to sell, you're well on your way to developing a successful marketing strategy.

Now you should ask yourself, "Why me?" Why should someone buy from you instead of buying from someone else? When a customer goes out to buy something, he is trying to fill a need. If you want to make the sale, you have to be the one who best fills that need. That's how you compete in the marketplace.

When Barkley & Evergreen gets a new client, one of the first things I do is invite their management team to my office for a game of cards. When I play cards with clients, I bring my own deck. The deck was originally developed by some gentlemen at Arthur D. Little who later refined the concept at The Berwick Group, Inc., in Boston. It's a deck of 23 cards and each card describes a different basis of competition. On pages 76–98, you'll find an enlarged version of each card. You should carefully review each basis and pick out the five that best describe how your company currently competes in the marketplace. While you're at it, have other people in your company do the same exercise. I often find senior managers within the same company who don't agree.

When I conduct this exercise for companies, we spend a great deal of time trying to reach a consensus. The way I go about it is to moderate a discussion which causes everyone participating to agree on a final three bases that they select from all their answers. The most important part of this exercise is the discussion that takes place about why certain cards should get discarded while others are retained.

After we've done that, I have everyone go through the cards a second time to pick out five ways they'd like to compete in the future. This portion of the exercise really has two parts. First, we have a discussion, as we did before, where we come to a consensus on the three bases that we want to use in the future. Then, the strategic part of the meeting begins when we try to develop ways in which we will move from the old bases of competition to the future. (Usually, only one or two of the new bases of competition are different from the current three bases that were agreed upon.) By the time this card game is over, we're on our way to developing their long-term marketing strategy. (At the bottom of each card, I've included an example of a company that uses that basis of competition.)

• Marketing is about what people buy, not what you sell.

> If you'd like a deck of cards, write to me at
> Barkley & Evergreen, 4350 Shawnee Mission
> Parkway, Fairway, KS 66205. Include $5.00 per
> deck for shipping and handling.

BASIS OF COMPETITION #1

Convenience

The customer is influenced by:

- Physical proximity
- Inventory strength
- Availability
- Ability to examine/purchase in a convenient time frame

EXAMPLE: 7-ELEVEN

Variety

The customer is influenced by:

- Breadth of selection
- Difference in style, color, etc.
- Difference in price ranges
- Variety of brands

EXAMPLE: KELLOGG'S
VARIETY PACK

Service

The customer is influenced on the basis of at least equal product and a believable and important service differentiation.

- Delivery
- Installation
- Availability of credit
- Repairing
- Education or training
- Guarantees or warranties

EXAMPLE: SEARS KENMORE

Personal Selling

The customer is influenced by the skill of the direct sales force, manufacturers' representatives, or dealer outlets; particularly when the product is:

- Complex
- Custom
- Expensive

EXAMPLE: ELECTROLUX
VACUUM CLEANERS

Product

The customer is influenced on the basis of some believable and important product features:

- Differentiated performance
- Peripheral features
- Versatility
- Customization
- Durability
- Ease of use

EXAMPLE: NIKON CAMERAS

Segmentation

The customer is influenced on the basis of successful identification of a market niche that others have not recognized or adequately filled.

EXAMPLE: TOPOL SMOKER'S TOOTHPASTE

Quality

The customer is influenced on the basis that your product line is of better quality than the competition in:

- Appearance
- Performance
- Results

EXAMPLE: MAYTAG

Price

The customer is influenced
on the basis of a lower price
since you and your competitors'
product and marketing mix
are essentially undifferentiated.

EXAMPLE: WAL-MART

Brand Name/ Image/Reputation

The customer is influenced by:

- Fashionability
- Quality
- Prestige
- Reliability

and other characteristics which he wants to associate with a particular purchase.

EXAMPLE: DOM PERIGNON

Advertising

The customer is influenced by how well his information needs are met through:

- Media: Newspapers, TV, radio, magazine, direct mail
- Point-of-sale: self-displaying cartons, etc.

EXAMPLE: BUDWEISER

Special Relationships

The customer is influenced by:

- Personal contact and availability
- Policy assistance
- Interchange of information
- Sales coordination
- Trade association affiliation

EXAMPLE: TUPPERWARE

Distribution Channels

The customer is influenced by the type, size, and location of the distribution system.

EXAMPLE: LAND'S END

Proof of Claims

The customer is influenced by the proof of major and/or secondary claims about the product, including warranties and guarantees.

EXAMPLE: EDDIE BAUER

BASIS OF COMPETITION #14

Product Breadth

The customer is influenced by broadness of the line, as it allows him to select items that fit his needs more exactly.

EXAMPLE: NIKE

Product Customization

The customer is influenced on the basis of creating a personalized version of the product:

- Full or semi-customization

EXAMPLE: TOM JAMES (CUSTOM-MADE MEN'S SUITS)

BASIS OF COMPETITION #16

Noncommercial Forms of Information

The customer is influenced by:

- Pronouncements of public figures
- Editorial content of news media
- Word of mouth
- Research

EXAMPLE: JELLY BELLIES JELLY BEANS (RONALD REAGAN)

Packaging

The customer is influenced by the package:

- Graphics
- Performance
- Physical characteristics
- Labeling

EXAMPLE: L'EGGS HOSIERY

Promotion

The customer is influenced by:

- Samples
- Coupons
- Price packs
- Related item promotions
- Trade allowances

EXAMPLE: PROCTER & GAMBLE

Merchandising

The customer is influenced by:

- Buying policies
- Pricing policies
- Discounts and allowances
- Cooperative advertising
- Mass floor displays
- Out-of-position displays
- Related item displays

EXAMPLE: *TV GUIDE*

Regulatory Social Compliance

The customer is influenced by:

- Adherence to regulatory guidelines
- Social responsibility
- Full financial disclosure

EXAMPLE: NYSE

Market Research

The customer is influenced by the manufacturer's knowledge about who is buying the product in terms of:

- Income
- Education
- Occupation
- Repeat purchase rate

EXAMPLE: NIELSEN RATINGS

Technology

The customer is influenced by technological innovation, patents, and proprietary products.

EXAMPLE: POLAROID

Physical Distribution

The customer is influenced by close attention to rapid resupply of distributor stocks and heavy inventories at all levels, or by strong emphasis on keeping dealers well supplied with minimum inventory cost to him.

EXAMPLE: JUST IN TIME DELIVERIES

THOU SHALT PUT IT IN WRITING AND PRODUCE IT IN TRIPLICATE

WHETHER YOU ALREADY manage thousands of people or you aspire to manage a few, you've got to have good communication skills to be successful. To a lot of business people, good communication simply means writing concise memos, producing professional reports, and documenting everything that happens. Or, in other words, keeping the paper flowing around the office.

I call that mentality CYA, meaning "Cover Your Ass." It describes people who feel like they have to document everything. They need evidence and excuses, so they can pass the blame if and when catastrophe strikes. In that type of environment, people must provide a record of every action, statement, and idea.

This is not to say that we don't need documentation in business. Every office has to keep some records. You need them for reference and for clarification. But that's where the utility of paper ends. As a means of communicating between yourself and others, writing stinks. Putting paper between you and other people makes communication impersonal. It also makes the message less effective. The most effective form of office communication is, and always will be, a good old-fashioned face-to-face talk. (That's why I also feel more effective in my seminars than I do writing a book.)

In advertising, people spend a lot of money on research just to find the best way to reach their audience. The decision of whether to run ads on television, in magazines, in newspapers, on the radio, or through direct mail is crucial to the success of advertising. Even though there are so many choices available today, almost any advertiser would agree that the ideal medium (if cost were no object) through which to sell their product or service would be the original one: talking to customers in person.

I'm a salesman. When I have something to sell, I like to do it eyeball to eyeball. If every advertiser could use this kind of personal selling on every customer, he'd have it made. But it's obviously impossible. So advertisers have to settle for second best and filter their messages through other media. But advertising is still a poor substitute for personal selling.

You're lucky. You can talk to everyone in your office. And they can talk to you. So why would you settle for anything less?

If you want to be a great communicator, you need to make sure that your office or department is a place where people aren't afraid to talk to each other. A good manager speaks to his coworkers, and they speak to him.

WHERE'S THE SUGGESTION BOX?

There's an office fixture that tells a lot about the kind of communication you'll find in a company. This device will also tell you a lot about management's view of employee participation in corporate communication. Of course, I'm talking about the proverbial suggestion box. You can really send a message to everyone simply on the basis of where you locate it.

At the Wolf Creek Golf Links, the ninth hole is a 415-yard par four. Both sides of the fairway are lined with trees. If you go into the woods, to the right of the fairway, about 150 yards from the green, and look up, you will see the club's suggestion box. It's nailed to one of the trees about 25 feet off the ground. Obviously, they don't check it too often.

Most companies aren't as straightforward as Wolf Creek. But all suggestion boxes send out a message about how a company feels about suggestions.

There is no reason why any office needs to have an employee suggestion box. It's not particularly conducive to open communication. If someone wants to make a suggestion or a comment, he should bring it to a person—not a box.

Some managers believe that employees will be intimidated and keep quiet if they have to identify themselves when they make a suggestion. If that describes your situation, you have a problem much deeper than the suggestion box. You're working in an office where people aren't comfortable speaking their minds.

Suggestion boxes should be called "suggestion screens." That's what they're used for—to filter OUT ideas. Only when an idea is considered a good one does a manager take the time to talk to the author. The problem is that when people's ideas are screened out, so are the people who thought of them. And when most of the people who do put their ideas in the box don't get any feedback, do you think they'll want to submit anything again?

When someone in your company has an idea or a suggestion, you ought to want them to run to your office to tell you about it. And you should encourage the people who report to you to do just that.

Suggestions are healthy, whether you use them or not. People feel a sense of ownership toward their suggestions, and they're proud when they come up with good ones. Suggestions take creativity. They show that people have been doing extra thinking about your business. It shows they care. Furthermore, people want to give these suggestions to you at no extra charge. What more could you ask?

At many Japanese companies, the number of suggestions received on a per-employee basis is an indicator of how the company's doing. If they don't get several hundred suggestions per employee per year, they think they have a problem.

At our office, we encourage everyone to take pride in their ideas and suggestions. In fact, we even give a $50.00 prize for the best suggestion each month, called the Big Idea of the Month Award. One winner suggested that we add a health-food vending machine to the cafeteria. Another big idea was to honor the mothers and fathers in the organization on Mother's Day and Father's Day.

A suggestion doesn't have to save thousands of dollars to be a good one. But more important than the suggestions themselves is that the people who submit them do it in person.

One of the best ways to measure the strength of your department or company is to look at how candid people think they can be with management. If they're not comfortable telling you what's wrong and how they'd suggest fixing it, a suggestion box will only mask your problem.

You need to create an environment in which no one is afraid to tell the emperor that he has no clothes.

Here's a method for communicating your desire for everyone to be forthcoming, and I guarantee it will dramatically change the way people perceive you. First, if you have your name on your office door, take it off. Next, replace it with a sign that reads:

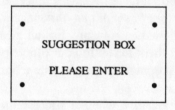

WHAT'S ON THE AGENDA?

One way we try to communicate with people is through meetings. I have two things to say about meetings. First, the number of meetings you hold is not necessarily related to the quality of communication in your office. Second, the types of meetings you hold are.

One of the best ways I know of to keep the channels of communication open between you and your staff is to have "small employee meetings." I have them every month. These are not gatherings of my cohorts—people under 5'8". By small employee meetings, I refer to informal meetings with five to seven other company employees that are nonmanagement.

Why do I need to hold small employee meetings? After all, I already hold regular staff meetings, get regular reports from department heads on their meetings, and speak to people individually all the time.

For starters, staff meetings are no place for discussion. I'm a firm believer in monthly staff meetings—to cover general information and to serve as a pep rally. The problem is that in most meetings, only a few people do any talking. I've always allowed for questions and comments at the end of our monthly general staff meetings. Except for a few jokes from some of the more seasoned veterans, almost no one makes a peep.

I've got some theories as to why this is so: some people are afraid of asking a stupid question or sounding like a brown-noser; or they think that others, who have a deadline to meet, will resent them for prolonging the meeting. Some people are just too intimidated to talk in front of large groups. Whatever the reasons, the general staff meeting is not the best forum for discussion.

At the other extreme are one-on-one meetings. These aren't any better for discussion. Unless you manage just one or two people, some of your staff may be intimidated. They might not be honest with you, for fear of saying the wrong thing.

So I found a cozy spot somewhere between the extremes. Small employee meetings are small enough to encourage contributions from everyone present, but big enough to offer timid folks some moral support.

I don't invite just anybody to these meetings; other than myself, no senior managers are allowed. Each month, I invite a few people from every department. I keep track of who comes and I make sure that everyone gets a turn.

Most people think that if you're going to hold a successful meeting, you've got to prepare an agenda. I disagree. Every month, I hold my one-hour small employee meeting without preparing anything. That's because everyone else brings their own agenda. In fact, that's what makes these meetings work so well. The whole meeting is devoted to what they want to cover. The ball's in their court. Usually, people go around their departments ahead of time to see if anyone has any questions or issues they want to raise with me. I hear it goes something like this: "Got anything you want to ask Fromm?"

Whatever happens, the discussions allow me to get a good sense of how people feel about their jobs, and about the company. I also get a chance to hear suggestions. But more importantly, I can get to know everybody a little better.

The people in our company also gain a lot from small employee meetings. They have an opportunity to give suggestions and complaints straight to the boss. Or they might ask me to clarify a rumor. It's also a great time to ask questions that may not seem important enough to ask under other circumstances.

If someone comes to me with a suggestion in one of these meetings, I may not make a snap decision. But something will happen soon. And if someone asks a question that I don't know the answer to, I write it down and make a point of finding out.

Even if you manage only a few people, you should still hold small employee meetings. You can sit down with the handful of people that you manage for an hour every month. If you only manage one or two people, you're not off the hook either. The important thing is that you don't have an agenda: they do.

An employee with entrepreneurial aspirations once asked, "What's the most important thing to know about running your own company?" This was a tough question. There were so many different things that I wanted to tell her. I then realized that she was already doing the most important thing. She was eager to ask questions, listen, and learn what other people had to say. If you want to be a successful leader, it sure helps to find out what other people think. Especially the people who know the most about your business—your employees.

"IT TAKES A LICKING AND KEEPS ON TICKING"

If I've convinced you that talking to people is the best form of communication, then I'd like to give you a tip on how to go about it. The first step is as simple as asking people, "What time is it?"

You see, there are two types of communicators, and I characterize them by the answers they give to that question.

One type responds by telling you that his watch is two minutes fast, although he hasn't checked it against an accurate watch in over a month. He then tells you that it's 11:34 and 42 seconds. I call people like him "watchmakers," because they practically tell you how their watch was made before they tell you the time.

The other type of communicator would snap back "11:30," and then be on his way. He's not concerned with what he perceives to be minor details. I call these people "tell-timers."

A watchmaker will explain something by starting at the very beginning. I mean the VERY beginning. In fact, often they start so far back in the story that you feel like you're waiting for them to get to the beginning. (That is, if you're not a watchmaker, too.)

A tell-timer's motor runs at a different speed. If you ask a tell-timer for the time, you'll get the time. You won't get a lengthy explanation. Just the time.

Several years ago, there was a personality conflict between a client's vice president and a vice president at our firm. Both people had high energy levels and were very bright. But, for some reason, they weren't getting along. Unable to figure out a solution, I had to resort to changing the person who handled the account.

A year later, after having been introduced to the concept of watchmakers and tell-timers, I called our vice president into my office to tell him that I had finally figured out the problem that he'd had a year ago. You see, he was a classic watchmaker and the client was a classic tell-timer. He hadn't been adapting his style to the client's style. He'd start his meeting or presentation at the VERY beginning. An hour later, he'd get to the part that the client was really there to hear—the recommendation. The client didn't want to review the strategy and objectives again before getting to the answer. He wanted a 20-minute meeting and we were taking two hours. We were trying his patience.

Once our vice president understood this—and I took plenty of time to explain it—he realized that to be more successful than he already was, he would have to do a better job of adapting his style to the person on the other side of the desk.

If you can adjust your style to the people with whom you're speaking, you can improve your ability to communicate and motivate.

The first step in improving your communication skills is recognizing what kind of communicator you are. Do you find yourself unsatisfied with short answers to questions? Do people often seem vague or unspecific? Do you take a lot of care when you speak to make sure that you're not misunderstood? If your answers to the above questions are predominantly "yes," then you're a watchmaker.

If, on the other hand, you find that people often take too long to answer questions, and you like people to be quick, then you're a tell-timer. As Joe Friday often said in *Dragnet*, "Just the facts, ma'am."

After you've established which type of communicator you are, you've got to learn how to adapt to the other type when you're talking to him. If you're a tell-timer talking to a watchmaker, try and be more detailed and more specific. If you're a watchmaker talking to a tell-timer, try to speak quickly, giving the minimum amount of information needed to get the job done.

When a watchmaker sits down in my office to go over something, the first thing that I do is lean back in my chair, take a deep breath, and try to relax. I'm trying to get prepared for a conversation that's going to take longer than I want. You see, if I rush a watchmaker, I may never find out what's really on his mind.

On the other hand, if a tell-timer walks into my office, I know that he probably won't even take a seat. He'll tell me what he wants and be gone before I can take that deep breath.

When I'm talking to a watchmaker, I know that I need to take it nice and easy. He's not going to be comfortable with a quick directive or a snap answer. If I'm talking to a tell-timer, I'm going to make my point and shut up. He'll get impatient if I take too much time.

Sometimes, you'll find yourself in a meeting with a lot of people, some of whom are watchmakers and some of whom are tell-timers. In that situation, try to find a pace somewhere in the middle. But, when you're answering questions, adapt your delivery to the person who asked the question. You'll know which type you're dealing with by the length and detail of the question.

As a manager, that's the best way to communicate with your people. But, you don't have to be a manager to want to communicate. If you're talking to your boss, try and adapt your style to his. The people in my organization who have the most success getting through to me are the people who adapt their styles to a tell-timer's pace. Even though I also try and adapt my style, it helps if the person on the other end is trying as well.

- Talking is three times better than writing in triplicate.
- If you want suggestions, get rid of your suggestion box.
- Don't tell people how to make a watch when they only want the time, AND don't tell people the time when they want to know how to make a watch.

THOU SHALT COVET NEW CUSTOMERS

WE IN ADVERTISING meet a lot of people who want to see their businesses grow. They come to an advertising agency because they believe that advertising is the best way to do that. They want to attract hordes of new customers. That's understandable. Every business needs a steady supply of customers to stay afloat.

I told you before that our agency is in the business of increasing clients' market share. But, I'm the first to admit that increasing the number of customers you have is not necessarily the best way to do that. It's a lot more profitable to increase your business with current customers.

When I started in the advertising business, my focus was almost exclusively on the automotive aftermarket. My clients were companies that manufactured replacement parts for automobiles. Though I didn't want to give up our company's specialty, I did want to diversify the clientele. However, it's not easy for an unestablished advertising agency to get new accounts.

We got a big break when the largest advertising agency in town resigned a small real estate company that they thought had no future. The real estate firm consisted of three people—a married couple and their son. It was located in the basement of a bank building.

That small real estate company was ERA. They did more than just grow—they exploded. As they grew, their advertising budget grew. And since they were happy with our services, they just kept doing more and more business with us.

ERA grew from that small company in a basement to the second largest real estate network in the world. We at Barkley & Evergreen grew with them and profited from their growth.

Your current customers represent your best opportunity for increased profits. Let's say you're a manufacturer of men's clothing. In the past year, you sold $100,000 worth of suits to one of your customers, a retailer. They happen to be a pretty good customer. However, they don't buy any of your dress shirts.

Rather than trying to find "new" dress shirt customers, go back and talk to that current suit customer. Selling him $20,000 worth of dress shirts next year will be a lot more profitable than finding a new $20,000 customer.

Here's why. If you increase your business by 20 percent with an old customer, you'll still have only one account receivable. Your salesman can handle this increase in business with the same sales call. Your freight costs will probably be less than shipping to a new customer. In every respect, this 20-percent increase in business from your existing customer will be more profitable than a similarly sized new account. McDonald's figured this out a long time ago. That's why they ask you if you also want fries or pies.

If this is all so obvious, why are so many companies focused on new business instead of selling current customers? Basically, there are two reasons.

First, selling additional products or services to existing customers lacks much of the "thrill of the kill" that one feels when "knocking off" a new customer. For someone who truly enjoys and thrives on selling, getting a new customer is a feeling that is hard to duplicate.

Second, getting additional business from an existing customer requires that you deliver exceptional service. In some ways, prospects are easier to sell because they haven't yet experienced beyond the honeymoon. With current customers, promises made have to be kept. Focusing on selling current customers will help discipline everyone in your firm toward delivering on those promises.

In advertising, as well as many other industries, we rarely make any money on a client during our first year with them. It's expensive to find new clients and to get our relationships running smoothly.

The only way that our company can make money is to find clients, keep them, and grow them. That's why it's so important to make sure that we're providing the absolute best customer service.

If you want to grow your business, you should do the same.

IS YOUR ACCOUNT OVERDRAWN?

You may be wondering exactly what it means to increase your customer service. If your customers seem content—if you're providing them with every service they expect from you—you may think you've got it covered. You may be wrong.

Excellent customer service reaches beyond what is required of your business. Just because no one else in the industry bothers with a certain practice doesn't mean you shouldn't be doing it. In fact, that extra touch may be just the thing you need to earn lifelong customers. What do I mean by extra touches?

When was the last time your lawyer called just to see how things are going? Probably never. My friend Gunther Klaus believes that the legal profession got its start during the Crusades. After the battle, the first lawyers were sent in to spear the wounded. That's a common perception of lawyers, because the only time they talk to you is when you're in trouble. Couldn't a lawyer stand out by taking the time to dispel that myth and showing a genuine interest in his clients?

Has your banker ever called you just to see how things were going? Probably not. That's why I consider most bankers to be a commodity—just another undifferentiated service. A banker could differentiate himself just by making a few phone calls to customers to see how things are going. But few do.

They're making a big mistake. Stephen Mulvaney, president of Management Tools, Inc., had done business with a bank for many years. They never called him or provided him with any service that wasn't expected of them.

One day, they made an error. He pointed it out and then switched banks. Someone from his old bank called and asked why he changed banks. After all, it was just one mistake.

He told them: "Let me explain this in a way you'll understand. A customer relationship is like a savings account. Every time you call a customer, send him a note to thank him for his business, or take other steps to service him, you are making deposits into that account. In every relationship, you're going to make mistakes, and when you do, the client makes a withdrawal on the account. If you haven't made any deposits, the first mistake causes the account to be overdrawn."

Think for a moment about the times you talk to customers. Do you tend to talk to customers only when they initiate the call? If your answer to this question is yes, you're one mistake away from being overdrawn.

You see, customers normally only initiate calls when they have a problem. And their problem dominates the agenda. You end up on the defensive, trying to hip-shoot your way out of a situation. That's no way to build a healthy relationship. What's worse, the customer may begin to believe that you never think of him except when he interrupts your work.

There's a saying in the advertising business that the first day you get a client is the first day you start to lose it. Someday that customer will leave you and go buy from someone else. Your mission is to avoid that day as long as you can. To do that, you need to build a relationship that can withstand the little mistakes that inevitably happen.

Most people who say they're in the service business give lousy service. And, those who are in retailing, distribution, or manufacturing need to understand that they're also in the service business. Without some kind of control over customer contact, you can't possibly maintain a relationship.

IT'S YOUR CALL

Instead of providing reactive service, start servicing customers before you're overdrawn. You don't want to be left saying, "But it was our first mistake." You've got to be on the offensive. You should be the one initiating the call. That way, you can plan ahead what you want to discuss. But more importantly, the customer will begin to see that you really care.

One of the most successful executives I've ever known is Richard Black. He was the president of Maremont Corporation in Chicago and was a client of mine. He turned that company around.

Rick had hundreds of customers. Instead of only calling customers when there was a problem, he'd call them on a regular basis just to visit. If he was waiting in the airport, he called clients. Even when Rick had news worthy of the press, his clients always had the inside scoop. By being proactive and thoughtful, Rick made all of his clients feel special. Rick Black had hundreds of customers who felt they were his best friend.

You can do it, too. First, you have to decide that you want to have proactive relationships with your customers instead of reactive ones. Next, put together a list of every person from every company with whom you want to maintain regular contact. Write down how often you'd like to talk to them on the phone and how often you'd like to visit them in person. This is your opportunity to determine the frequency of customer contact rather than have it be a function of how often your customer calls you with a problem. Now spread this list of names over a year-long schedule. Some of the people you may want to call as often as once or twice a week; others you may need to talk to only once or twice a year.

Then, each week, call the people on your list. During some of the calls, you can plan upcoming visits. But the purpose behind all of them is to let customers know that you're happy to have their business, and to ask:

How are things going?

Is there anything else we can do for you?

PUT OUT A WELCOME MAT

I'm always looking for ways to make customers feel more comfortable with our company. You have to, if you want to maintain outstanding customer service.

Several years ago, I went to see a new client at his office for the first time. When I arrived, I saw my name up on the message board, welcoming me as a visitor. I was a supplier, not a customer—and I was impressed. They were awaiting my arrival. This extra attention made me feel good about being there, and it made the trip seem more worthwhile.

The most important words to any person are his name. And, there are few things that feel as good as seeing your name in lights. Maybe that's why some actors and their agents spend so much time negotiating top billing—more time, in fact, than they spend negotiating salaries.

We have a message board at our receptionist's desk. It wasn't any stroke of genius on my part. I put it there as soon as I got back from that client. We use it to welcome our clients. If they feel the same way that I do, seeing their names up there makes them feel special and welcome. They know we're glad that they're visiting— and we are.

If your company is too large for one message board, you can put one in your department. You can welcome customers, suppliers, and even fellow employees from other departments that you want to impress.

The cost of this little touch is less than negligible. But it means a heck of a lot to a client who traveled all day to get to your office.

HERE'S JOHNNY!

There's an important side benefit to posting greetings in your reception area. Since everyone in the company passes the board when they get to work, they all know if a client is going to be in the office that day. If they see him in the hall, they can call him by name.

The fact of the matter is that a person likes to hear his name even more than he likes to see it. How do you think Ed McMahon kept his job on "The Tonight Show" so long?

HOW TO MAKE FRIENDS IN HIGH PLACES

Some of your clients may have secretaries or receptionists. They can either help you or hinder you in your attempts to keep your client happy. Their job is to help their boss get his work done by screening, prioritizing, and shutting the door on those who want to see him. That's why I refer to them as "gatekeepers." I have one, too. I tell people that she runs my office in my name. That's not far from the truth.

Few people can boast the amount of power and influence that a secretary can. That's why you have to do your best to keep them happy.

Secretaries are vital to your success. A secretary can get you through to the boss or help ensure that he returns your call. I've had the good fortune to be on the receiving end of these favors more than a few times. One day, I desperately needed to talk to one of my clients. His secretary knows his schedule down to the minute. The first time I could talk to him was at 3:40 PM. I was going to be on an airplane until then. He was supposed to go into a meeting at 3:30. She agreed to delay him eleven minutes until I could call.

On National Secretaries Day, she received a dozen roses from me with a note that read: "For all you do, this bud's for you."

I give all of my clients' secretaries roses on National Secretary's Day. The day is probably a plot devised by the National Association of Secretaries and the floral companies to take advantage of people like me. But who cares? They came up with a good opportunity to thank some of the most important people I deal with.

DEATH OF A SALESMAN

If you want to ensure that your current clients are receiving the kind of attention they deserve, you need to know something about the people in your sales force. And, if you happen to be a member of a sales force, you need to know something about yourself. Let me explain with a history lesson.

It dawned on a caveman one day that everyone in his tribe would be better off if there were a division of labor. It occurred to him that some people should do the hunting and some people should do the skinning. What a concept. Division of labor made most tasks much easier and freed up time for the development of technology. At the time, high-tech was learning how to build a better mammoth trap.

Today, division of labor is everywhere. But most companies' sales forces haven't gotten the picture yet.

If you look at the selling process from a macro view, you'll see that selling involves two basic types of skills that are quite different. The first skill required is the one that enables the sales person to do everything from making a cold call to closing the sale. A different skill is required to keep the customer well-serviced and happy over a long period of time. It's been my observation, as well as my personal experience as a salesman, that the two basic skills required for selling are not usually found in the same person.

A sales person is by nature either a hunter or a skinner. Hunters are the sales people who love to get on the phone or get into their cars and make cold calls. The thrill for a hunter is the hunt. If you ask a hunter what it feels like to close a sale, he might even equate it to an orgasmic experience. I know, because I'm a hunter.

Skinners are people who love developing longterm relationships with their customers. Although they find cold calling intimidating, they love to spend time with customers. In fact, skinners usually have lots of customers as personal friends.

If you've ever tried to manage a sales force, you know that you need both hunters and skinners if you're going to succeed. Every business needs to have a continuous supply of new customers in order to grow. But, in addition to adding new customers, you've also got to keep your current customers happy and keep their business growing with you.

The problem is that in most companies both types of sales people are asked to do both types of jobs.

If people aren't comfortable with something, they won't do a great job, no matter how hard they try. Do you have any idea what it's like for a skinner to make a cold call? It's frightening, to say the least. Most skinners will go out of their way to avoid that kind of situation. In fact, they'll drive right by a new prospect on the way to see their oldest customer and best friend.

Hunters, on the other hand, get bored to tears servicing existing customers. They just want to make the new sale and go on to the next kill. Ask one of your customers what kind of service he's getting from a hunter who's still calling on him, and you won't be very happy with what you hear.

When you ask hunters to skin and skinners to hunt, you're not taking advantage of their strengths. To the extent that a hunter spends time skinning, the company is wasting his ability to attract new customers. Conversely, time spent by a skinner in hunting is not as productive as it could be, because he won't have as high a "kill rate" as a hunter, and he won't have time to provide the kind of service to an existing account that would result in increased sales and customer loyalty.

If you really want to maximize your sales productivity, let hunters hunt and skinners skin. Here's how to do it.

First of all, recognize that it takes far fewer hunters in a sales organization than it does skinners. One good hunter can support scads of skinners. If you deploy your sales people on a geographical basis, you may be able to have one hunter covering a broad area that includes the territories of anywhere from three to ten skinners, depending on the maturity of the market. On the other hand, if your market penetration isn't too good in a particular part of the country, you may have one hunter working the same area as one skinner.

Hunters don't have to be organized on a geographical basis at all. They could be organized by product line, by type of industry served, or even by the personality profile of the prospective customer. Skinners, on the other hand, need to be organized geographically so that they can be close to the customer.

DON'T DECLAW A LION

One situation that occurs in many companies is that the sales manager comes from the ranks of the hunters, while most of the sales force are skinners. There are two obvious problems with this.

First, most hunters make terrible sales managers. The skills needed for sales management are quite different from the skills needed for successful hunting. Hunters tend to be very impatient. Skinners, on the other hand, are natural managers. They're pros at taking care of people and treating them like family. That's what skinning is.

The second problem is that when a hunter is promoted to a sales management position, he is forced to leave the "jungle" and rarely returns to the hunt again. This results in a decline in the new business effort.

One way to solve these problems is to avoid mixing hunters and skinners. Skinners should report to a sales manager who's a skinner. Hunters, on the other hand, can either report to a sales manager who's a hunter who still occasionally hunts; or if there are only a few hunters, they can report to the head of marketing or even the CEO.

I can't leave this point without emphasizing the fact that hunters are NOT more important than skinners. It follows, then, that hunters should not necessarily make more money than skinners. It takes both types of sales people, working at what they do best, for a company to maximize its full potential.

ADVERTISING CAN KILL YOUR BUSINESS

When you can't provide outstanding customer service for your customers, you don't want new ones.

Barnett Helzberg is chairman of the board of a chain of retail mall jewelry stores called Helzberg Diamonds. Barnett's company has been a client of ours for a number of years. I've taught him a few things about advertising, and he's taught me when not to advertise.

Our company had developed a rather sophisticated software program for retailers that owned stores in a number of markets. This program told them the best way to allocate their advertising media funds, based on the return they could expect. Some markets offered a greater return on advertising investment than others, and it didn't necessarily have to do with the size of the market or the number of stores the retailer had in the market. The first time we used this program with Barnett's company, I went with our media director to present our findings. We presented a series of charts and graphs that clearly showed what the relative advertising weight ought to be for each of the Helzberg markets.

Barnett was impressed. However, he insisted that we add another factor before we made our final decision on the allotment of advertising dollars. He thought that there was no point in spending money in markets where they didn't have the right people in place.

In any large retail organization, occasionally a store may not have the right management in place, or the sales people may not be properly trained or motivated. They aren't prepared to give outstanding customer service. In that case, Barnett understood that there's no point in advertising. It would probably hurt business more than it helped.

ASK OGILVY

In *Confessions of an Advertising Man*, David Ogilvy covers the topic of advertising shoddy products. "If I try hard enough, I can write an advertisement which will persuade consumers to buy inferior products, *but only once*—and most of my clients depend on repeat purchases for their profit." He goes on to quote Howard Morgens, " 'The quickest way to kill a brand that is off in quality is to promote it aggressively. People find out about its poor quality just that much more quickly.' "

Advertising can't be the fuel that runs your company. It can only give you a jump start. The driving is up to you. Keep both hands on the wheel.

You have to provide your customers with the best service possible. It won't suffice to lure them in with great service and cut it off. You'll only lose them. If it comes to that, you'll need a steady flow of new customers just to make up for the steady flow that's leaving.

If someone does you the service of buying from you, do him the courtesy of taking good care of him. Don't go looking for new

customers until you're certain that your old ones are getting the
attention they deserve. If you can't manage to keep your current
customers happy, you certainly aren't ready for new ones.

A BUSINESSMAN'S DREAM

There's a payoff for all of this attention to your customers—aside
from their continued loyalty and business.

   Imagine a product or service so good that your customers are
your missionaries. They go around telling people how great you
are. Stroud's restaurant in Kansas City is that kind of business.
They refer to themselves as "the home of pan-fried chicken."
Their motto, "We choke our own chickens," appears on their
T-shirts. People come in, have a great time, fall in love with the
food, and tell all their friends about it. Stroud's doesn't spend a
dime on advertising. In fact, they make money on their T-shirts.
Hidden behind a freeway overpass with no parking lot, Stroud's
may have the worst location in Kansas City. Nonetheless, the place
is always packed. In fact, it's not unusual for people to wait over
two hours. For fried chicken, mind you.

   • Old customers are more profitable than new ones.
   • Call your customers before they find you.
   • Let hunters hunt and skinners skin.
   • Nothing kills a bad product faster than good advertising.

Thou Shalt Have Rules

WE DON'T HAVE a dress code in our office. There's nothing written in a dusty volume somewhere that says what you can or cannot wear to work. One day, a woman came to work in cutoff shorts and tennis shoes with no socks. It caused quite a stir—even in an advertising agency, where we're overdressed in wingtip shoes. The manager of her department came to warn me before I saw her. He suggested, as he had in the past, that we really needed a dress code.

I explained to him that 95 percent of our staff came to work looking just fine—without a dress code. How would these people feel if we suddenly started treating them like children, just because one person didn't use good judgment? Instead of imposing a dress code, I arranged a meeting with the woman and suggested that she try a slightly less informal look in the future. It was a little embarrassing for both of us, but it worked.

What would I have done if it hadn't worked? I still wouldn't have imposed a dress code. I would probably have tried a more serious talk with the woman who was using such poor judgment. I would have explained why we don't have rules and how that doesn't mean that I want people showing up in beach attire.

I'd have also asked her if there was something else bothering her. Something that was happening at the office or at home that was upsetting her. Was she happy with her job? That's how you solve a problem—not with rules. It's amazing how many problems you can clear up by talking. I never want to work with a person with whom I can't sit down and talk.

I'll confess that I've always had an aversion to rules. They're not the answers to problems; they're more like Band-Aids. Someone once said, "A rule is a scar from a previous bad experience." Amen.

I tend to be a free spirit. I wouldn't enjoy working somewhere that had a lot of rules. I prefer to use good, old-fashioned common sense.

Wouldn't you like to think that the people in your company have enough common sense to act reasonably? If they don't, it's a reflection on you—you probably hired them, or hired the person who hired them. And, they're making decisions which will affect the welfare of the business. If you don't think they have common sense, then they shouldn't be working for you.

A big problem with rules is that they don't allow for flexibility.

A company offered customers a free quart of oil for any purchase over $25.00, excluding tires. (Tire purchases always amounted to much more than $25.00.) One customer demanded the free quart of oil, even though the purchase had been tires.

"I spent more than $25.00, and I expect the oil!" the customer shouted.

The clerk actually argued with the customer because the customer wasn't following the rules. The customer had spent a lot of money. Who cares about the rules in a case like this? Had the rule not been imposed, the clerk would probably have decided to go ahead and give him the free quart of oil. This would have placated the customer and avoided an unfavorable display at the checkout stand.

We don't want rules that send our customers running to our competitors—so why do we implement rules that send our staff into feelings of distrust, bitterness, and unhappiness?

An example of a widespread rule is office hours. Obviously, every company has to have office hours in order to operate effectively. But when office hours become rigid rules, common sense flies right out the window. Suppose your office hours are 8:00 AM to 5:00 PM, and let's assume these hours are strictly enforced. What are you, as a manager, going to do when a staff member who's salaried and not paid for overtime wants to work past 5:00 PM to get something important done? Suppose the person works until 10:00 PM? Is he required to show up at 8:00 AM the next morning? And if you make an exception, where do the exceptions stop?

The best policy manual I've heard of is at Worthington Industries, a major steel producer in Columbus, Ohio. Their entire policy manual is on one page. It says that you should treat your customers and fellow employees the same way that you want to be treated.

Most company policy manuals are thicker than the flight plan for a space shuttle mission. What for? Just use common sense.

I do have one rule. I call it the 95/5 rule: Don't make rules to govern the 5 percent of your staff who do it wrong when 95 percent of your staff do things right without rules.

WE RENT HELICOPTERS®

Whether the 95/5 rule will work for you depends on your corporate culture. Corporate culture is just like any other kind of culture—it encompasses traditions, environment, beliefs, practices, opinions, and much more. In general, it affects the way people feel about their work. Every company has a culture. If you don't want to have rules in your company, you've got to have the kind of culture that doesn't require them. In that kind of culture, people have their own high standards. In fact, in such a culture, people surpass your expectations.

On the other hand, there are cultures in which the people don't enjoy their work, and they do whatever they can to get around it. That kind of culture hinders productivity and creativity. If you have that kind of culture in your office, you probably need rules in order to maintain any semblance of order.

But rules are a superficial solution to such a problem. When you force people to conform to your standards, they aren't happy. Circulating a memo and laying down the law is not going to lift your people out of a rut. On the contrary, it'll give them one more reason to stay in it.

If you want to make a change, you have to go to the roots of the problem and change the culture. To give you a better idea of what a good culture is, I'd like to give you a couple of examples.

There was a bad winter storm in the western United States which caused an interruption in phone service. At Federal Express, that meant that no customers could call for pickups, and no mail could go through. Federal Express has an unconditional commitment to overnight delivery. To them, a problem with phone lines is no excuse.

An employee at Federal Express—a nonmanagement employee, I might add—drove to the phone company to find out what could be done about the problem. The phone company told him that it was a terrible storm (as if he didn't know that), and that the phone lines had become detached from the transformer that sat on top of a mountain outside of town. When he asked how long it would be before the problem was fixed, the phone company estimated three or four days.

Well, this nonmanagement employee knew that as long as the phone lines were down, no customers could call and no mail could get through. So he jumped into his car to drive to the top of the mountain to see if HE could fix the problem. The storm was so bad that his car couldn't make it and he was forced to turn back.

Wow! Can you imagine having employees who would try to drive to the top of a mountain in a snow storm? What's more, he made that decision on his own about a problem over which he had no control and which he was not responsible for fixing.

The problem with the phone lines hurt every business in town. But the employee at Federal Express was the one who took the initiative to fix it. Why? Because at Federal Express, every employee is encouraged to think and act independently. And they know that they have the responsibility and authority to do whatever is necessary to get the job done.

The amazing part is that the story isn't over. After he returned to town, he rented a helicopter to fly him to the top of the mountain. When they got there, the pilot couldn't find a place to land, so this employee of Federal Express jumped out of the helicopter into waist-high snow and trudged to the transformer where he proceeded to hook up the phone lines.

Tom Peters, coauthor of *In Search of Excellence* and other business bestsellers, tells this story. I first heard it when I was at one of his seminars. He points out that if an employee of almost any American company rented a helicopter on his own without having the title of chairman of the board and founder, he'd be history.

When I heard that story, I wondered what is it about Federal Express that makes their employees want to take so much responsibility for getting their work done. They set the standards for service in their industry.

It seemed that if I wanted to set the standards for service in advertising, I'd have to give our people the responsibility to exceed their authority.

In other words, our people have to feel comfortable taking care of customers even when it means exceeding the normal bounds of their authority. They have to feel comfortable renting helicopters. I started telling that story to the people at Barkley & Evergreen, and we adopted the slogan, We Rent Helicopters.®

This slogan has come to illustrate our corporate culture. The philosophy behind our culture is simple. We are committed to customer service and we realize that in order to fulfill that commitment we've got to give people the responsibility and authority to get the job done. This culture pervades our office and is known to our clients, suppliers, and employees.

To our clients, We Rent Helicopters® means that if they have a job that needs to be done, we will get it done. Even if we have to rent a helicopter.

To our people, We Rent Helicopters® means that if they are working on something for a client, they have the authority to do whatever it takes to complete the job correctly and on time. And, if that means renting a helicopter—so be it.

One important part of a company's culture is the way management recognizes employees who stand out. A company's employee recognition program should have everything to do with that company's culture. Each month, our management committee selects an employee as the winner of the Copter Club Award. This person is the one who best exemplifies the spirit of renting helicopters. He or she is recognized at our monthly staff meeting, and is given a plastic model helicopter (with a $100 bill inside) to hang from the ceiling of their office for the next month. The helicopter is then returned (sans the $100 bill) to be given to the next month's winner.

The monthly winners also receive a shirt with the Copter Club emblem on it and get their name on a permanent plaque that hangs in the office.

Each year, an annual winner is selected from the monthly winners to receive the Annual Copter Club Award. The person so honored gets a plaque; their name on a permanent trophy that sits in our reception area; and a one-week, all expense paid vacation for two. The one-week trip doesn't count as vacation time, either. The first year's winner won a trip to the Hawaiian island of her choice including airfare, meals, and a helicopter tour of the island. Other winners have been to Acapulco and Bermuda.

I can't tell you how many times I see someone in the office working late and when I ask him what he's doing, he tells me he's "renting a helicopter." Or, better yet, I just love it when a client calls me on the phone and starts the conversation off with: "Billy, I need you to rent me a helicopter." That means our company is going to get another opportunity to demonstrate superior customer service. It's part of our culture.

The point of all this is that employee-of-the-month awards and slogans are nice, but they usually lack the excitement and enthusiasm that management originally intended. If your employee programs can be tied into your corporate culture, you'll have planted the seeds for growing a high performance company. And, if you can develop a slogan that characterizes your entire corporate culture program, the people in your organization will be able to focus on the goal and objectives you've identified.

ONE RARE GORILLA®

Since we started "renting helicopters," a number of other companies have asked us to put similar programs together for them.

Lenny Hershman, a friend of mine and president of Passport Travel, was one of them. I knew Lenny pretty well. And I knew that he'd been taking annual trips to Rwanda to observe the rare silver-backed mountain gorillas. You'd remember them if you saw the movie *Gorillas in the Mist*—the true-life story of Dian Fossey. Anyway, Lenny has taken so many pictures of these gorillas that he's nearly covered his office walls with them.

What's the connection? Well, there are only 200 silver-backed mountain gorillas left today. And Lenny likes to say that great customer service is as rare as a silver-backed mountain gorilla.

So he set out to make the mountain gorillas and great customer service less rare through his new culture program.

First, he became a sponsor of the Digit Fund, started by Dian Fossey and adopted a silver-backed mountain gorilla named Ndatwa. Then he started One Rare Gorilla® in his company.

It started with a monthly award to the employee who gave the best customer service. When someone is named One Rare Gorilla®, he or she receives $100 cash, a limited-edition One Rare Gorilla® T-shirt, and a gift certificate for a dinner for two at one of Kansas City's finest restaurants. Perhaps more importantly, a giant stuffed gorilla sits in his or her office for a month, as testimony to the achievement. Customers can't help but become familiar with Passport Travel's culture; when they see that gorilla, they have to ask questions.

Time passed, and like all gorillas, One Rare Gorilla® evolved. Lenny wanted to keep it sacred, so he no longer awards it automatically every month. Instead, it's awarded on the spot—whenever it's warranted.

The enthusiasm for One Rare Gorilla® is infectious. There's a giant stuffed gorilla in the lobby and specially-made gorilla balloons in some of the offices. Employees wear small lapel pins with the logo, and various other gorilla paraphernalia—posters, stuffed toys, photos—are scattered around the place. It's a program that really sticks with the staff.

At most travel agencies, once the customer pays the bill, it's bon voyage. That's not the case at Passport Travel. Lenny knows that providing good service when there's no commission involved is the key to repeat business.

His "rare gorillas" know it, too.

One gorilla winner was a student in Passport's Travel School where travel agents are trained. She'd heard of a client who was going to cancel his cruise because he couldn't get a flight with a nonsmoking seat. (He had a serious respiratory problem.) She made a complicated series of phone calls, and was able to make the appropriate nonsmoking flight arrangements. Thanks to her, the customer was able to take the cruise.

Remember, she wasn't a travel agent yet. She was still in travel school, but she was obviously quite familiar with the One Rare Gorilla® philosophy.

Another One Rare Gorilla® award went to a travel agent who received a disturbing phone call from a regular client. He called to announce his suicide. The travel agent calmed him down by phone and was able to convince him to wait for her arrival. She sat with him for four hours that afternoon until his family arrived.

She knew when to stop worrying about selling plane tickets and when to take care of a more important customer need.

For the real stars, Passport Travel also has an annual award. The winner gets a trip for two to Rwanda for a one-rare-gorilla-meets-another-rare-gorilla camera safari.

SWITCHBOARD HOURS

After the seeds of your culture take root, you should start looking for things that you can do to nurture and help it grow. Our culture is based on our slogan, We Rent Helicopters®. And part of what "renting helicopters" means is working harder to service clients.

When it comes to servicing clients, any advertising agency can claim they work harder than their competitors. Proving it is something else. That's what we had in mind when we decided to lengthen the switchboard hours at Barkley & Evergreen.

In order to demonstrate our extraordinary devotion to service, we restructured the receptionists' schedules to keep the switchboard open from 7:00 AM to 6:00 PM. Then we sent a letter to all of our clients announcing the change. What we really sent was a clear message that we worked hard for our clients—two hours harder than most advertising agencies. The gesture was a small one, but we figured they'd appreciate the extra effort.

What we didn't figure was that the restructuring of the switchboard hours would bring about some unanticipated changes in work habits.

Time Flies When You're Having Fun

There's a tradition in America to mark the end of the day with a bell. We all spent a big chunk of our lives being herded around schools at the sound of a bell. It didn't matter if your math teacher was in the middle of long division; when the bell rang, it was time to go.

Well, old habits die hard. Most offices today are in the practice of sounding a "bell" at the end of the work day. I'm talking about the bell that rings when the switchboard goes to night answer and the phone rings. Time to tidy up your desk, put on your coat, and hit the road.

Others companies are a bit more technologically advanced. For example, some large corporations do their employees the service of providing a P.A. newsflash: "It is 4:45. The temperature is 74 degrees. The commuter trains are running on schedule . . ."

The cue in our office was typical. When the switchboard operator left at 5:00 PM, the phones were switched to a night answer system. Any incoming call after five o'clock elicited a melodic "bing bing" throughout the entire office. And the people remaining in the office inherited the responsibility of answering the phone.

When we decided to extend the switchboard hours for better client service, I announced it at our next staff meeting—just as a matter of course.

Immediately, people started coming to work earlier and leaving work later. I'm talking an *average* of 45 minutes earlier and 45 minutes later every day. And I'm talking about salaried employees. At first, I couldn't explain this phenomenon. People in my office have always had a tendency to work long hours, but this was a drastic jump. Then it dawned on me that people were reacting to the extended switchboard hours.

You see, the school bell wasn't ringing at the end of the day. People were wrapped up in their work and lost track of the time. They were busy, and no one was reminding them to leave when the clock struck five. And they didn't mind working later, because they didn't have the dreaded responsibility of answering the night bell, and running around the office to look for someone who had already left. They were no longer being penalized for working late.

In the morning, early arrivals were no longer faced with a dark, quiet office. People who happened to come in at 7:00 AM were rewarded with a smiling switchboard operator and a bright office. They were more willing to come in early, because they no longer had to raise the office from the dead.

Our culture was beginning to grow on its own. After I made the announcement that we were increasing the switchboard hours to demonstrate our superior service to clients, people were more willing to take the responsibility to provide that service. And since we stopped reminding people when it was time to leave, and stopped penalizing the people who were staying later than 5:00 PM, many people stopped their routine 5:00 PM exodus. They wanted to work harder in order to provide the best service—and did.

Is there something about your corporate culture that tells people that they have to leave at 5:00 PM? Maybe you could do something differently that would make it easier for people to work later. For one thing, you have to make it safe for people to leave the office at night. You might suggest putting in better lighting in the parking lot. Or maybe you need to provide cab vouchers for people who work after hours.

If someone wants to come in on a weekend, does he have a way to get into your building? These are all things that have to be considered if you want to make it easier for people to work extra hours.

ANYBODY HOME?

Several months after we changed our switchboard hours, our company was in competition with another local agency for a big piece of business. The prospect was getting ready to make his decision and agreed to a game of golf one Friday afternoon so we could "discuss possible marketing strategies."

As we were driving back to my office, I reassured him that my spending a workday at a country club with him did not reflect the work ethic at our office. In fact, I told him, "We work much harder than most other agencies." As could be expected, he was skeptical. So I proposed that he test my claim.

I suggested that he call the other agency from my car phone. It was then 5:50 PM on a Friday. I dialed my competition from the car phone, and my prospect listened on the speaker phone. The phone rang four times. It was answered by a machine, which, in an incredibly pleasant voice, informed us that the office hours were from 8:30 to 5:00, Monday through Friday.

I dialed my office, and the first ring was interrupted by a real live person saying, "Barkley & Evergreen."

I asked the receptionist to read me all of the names of the people who were still in the office. We keep a sign-out log. I cut her off somewhere in the "Ds" and asked her to give us a count. Almost half of the people were still there.

It was at this point that my prospect turned to me and said, "You've got the account."

THE TOUGHEST JOB YOU'LL EVER LOVE

It's easy to indoctrinate new employees into your culture. You should start when you've got their undivided attention—before they get the job.

I do. I sit down with every prospective employee before his first day to ensure that he understands our culture. My pep talk happens to be based on an old television commercial that accurately describes the advertising industry.

Think back to the mid-sixties. If you're too young to do that, play along with me, so I don't feel old. When John Kennedy started the Peace Corps, they ran an outstanding ad to entice young people to enlist.

The commercial opened with a scene in an underdeveloped country. An American in his mid-twenties walked behind a plow that was being pulled by an ox. As you watched him till the parched earth, an announcer began talking off camera. What he said went something like this:

"If you've just graduated from college and you're looking for a job halfway around the world where you can work in 120-degree heat, sleep on a dirt floor, take a chance of getting malaria, get paid $1.25 an hour, and feel better about yourself than you ever thought possible, have we got a job for you."

It worked. College graduates and grandmothers alike volunteered in such extraordinary numbers that the Peace Corps had a problem they had never anticipated. They had more Americans wanting to help than they had places to send them.

If you were interviewing for a position at our company and the supervisor decided to make you an offer, he'd tell you that before you could accept it, you'd have to meet with the president of the company—me.

We'd meet in my office on a Saturday morning. I like Saturday mornings because it sends a not-too-subtle message that we work a lot of hours.

I'd start off by congratulating you on your job offer. I'd try to put you at ease by telling you that we are NOT meeting so that I can pass final judgment on your qualifications. If you want the job, it's yours. I go on to tell you that the reason for our meeting is so that I can be sure that you understand the repercussions of the decision you're about to make. Then I launch into what I call my Peace Corps speech.

"We have incredibly high morale in this company. Because of that, I'm concerned that the people you met with might have painted a picture with a little more blue sky in it than should be there. I know that you currently have a good job, and I want to make sure that if you accept our offer, you're not going to be making a mistake.

"You should expect to work harder here than you ever have in your life. You're going to come to work early and leave late. You're going to work on weekends and even some holidays. You will find this environment extremely competitive, because the people here are the best in their field. You will probably find all of this very intimidating. By the end of your first month, you won't know whether you're going to quit or get fired.

"On the other hand, I want to make sure that you realize that you're going to have more fun than you ever thought you could have while you worked. It'll be 'the toughest job you'll ever love.' "

If you haven't walked out of my office yet, I go on to explain: "You're going to learn a lot about the advertising business. In fact, should you ever decide to leave, you'll probably be in a position to catch on with any other advertising agency. After all, once you've been a starter on a championship team, your value goes way up.

"But, the bottom line is, if you're not prepared to throw your body in front of a train, you're not ready for Barkley & Evergreen."

This indoctrination weeds out the people who don't love hard work. And it brings out the work ethic in borderline cases.

I received a phone call from a man I've known since high school. He wanted to apply for a job at Barkley & Evergreen. Since I didn't know if he was ready for hard work, I wasn't sure that this was the right place for him. So, as soon as he came in to see me, I gave him the old Peace Corps speech. It didn't seem to dissuade him much; he still had that idealistic twinkle in his eye.

So I put him to another test.

When he left, I called one of my department heads into my office. This man held a position similar to the one for which my old friend was applying. And, he had a travel schedule that would make a travel agent rich overnight.

"I like this guy a lot, but he just doesn't get it," I told the department head. "He doesn't realize the demands that will face him in this position. I want him to interview with you; take him through your calendar for a typical month and show him what you've been doing. Don't gloss over anything. In fact, tell him everything you hate about your job. Go in there and let him have it with both barrels."

After that interview, my friend popped into my office. "Can we talk a minute?" he said. We discussed his interview, and he said: "You weren't kidding. I need the weekend to think this over."

When decision time came, my friend said: "I've decided to take the job. But I'm real glad I had that last interview. Now I know what I'm getting into."

What you say to people before you hire them is a lot more important than what you say to them after they've already started working for you. When someone is interviewing for a job, he really listens. He's trying not to miss any clue that will help him say the right thing or give the right impression. You can use this attentiveness to your advantage; introduce him to your culture from the very start.

Be realistic, though. If you don't give the downside, you're going to unmotivate your new employee faster than you think.

I believe that you only have 30 days, at best, to indoctrinate a new employee into your culture. If you take longer than that, it probably isn't going to happen. Facing such a short window of opportunity, you should want to get a head start by beginning the process before day one.

Besides, by issuing the challenge while you have the prospective employee's undivided attention, you have a much better chance of finding Peace Corps material.

YOU NEVER FORGET YOUR FIRST DATE

The first day on the job makes a permanent impression on a new employee. That's why you can't afford to miss this opportunity to make the right impression.

I meet with every employee first thing in the morning of his first day. I want him to know how excited we are that he's now part of our organization. And to make sure that he gets that message, I want to give it to him myself. As manager, you have the clout to make a new employee feel important.

When I meet with him, I tell him the history of the company. I've seen plenty of beautiful brochures from very sophisticated companies that go into great detail about their history. But, I've never seen one that got someone pumped up to work.

I do what no brochure can do; I give him an oral history of our company. I go all the way back to the very beginning. It takes me about 30 or 40 minutes to bring him up to the present. And he has a chance to ask questions along the way.

Then, I tell him about our goals and objectives for the future. I want him to start sharing in our dreams. Again, I encourage questions because it helps break down some of the initial barriers.

Now, I'm ready to shift gears and give him his first assignment. I hand him a list of all of the employees in the company. After each employee's name is their title, department, and telephone extension. I tell the new person that he has to get every person at Barkley & Evergreen to initial this sheet within the next 30 days. If you work in a huge company, it may be wise to limit the list to the office or department in which the new hire will be working. Our agency has about 100 people; nonetheless, new employees still meet every one of them during the first month without any trouble.

The idea is not a novel one. You may remember doing the same thing if you pledged a college fraternity or sorority. The "pledge master" made this one of your first obligations. He wanted to be sure that you met and knew all of the members. After all, how could you ever build that all-important spirit if you didn't know everyone you'd be living with?

As a new employee makes his rounds to get his sheet initialed, he'll also have the opportunity to find out some of the unique things about the place. And, when he meets with department heads other than his own, they'll take a few extra minutes to tell him about their departments.

I finish this portion of our meeting by telling him that I want to be the last person to initial his sheet. This ensures that I'll be seeing him at least once more before a month has passed.

Next, he gets a copy of our company binder and I take him

through its contents. The first section contains the written policies of the company. Our goal with this section was to make it as short as possible. In fact, my dream is to someday have no written policy manual at all. The problem is that my attorney thinks my dream is a nightmare.

The next section of the binder is the client section. In it, he'll find a complete profile of every customer in our company. He can't be expected to give great customer service if he doesn't know a little something about who he is supposed to serve.

The next section contains biographies and pictures of all of our employees. We encourage everyone to get creative with their bios; some of them are outrageous.

Now, as we come to the end of our visit, I try again to encourage the new employee to ask questions. He doesn't feel so new anymore, and the questions and excitement start to build. Before he leaves, I remind him that I'll be seeing him again when he's ready for me to initial his "pledge sheet."

Depending on your position, and the setup of your company, you may want to modify your "first date" with your new employees. For example, if you manage one department, you could limit the names on the pledge sheet to your department. But, wouldn't it be nicer if you sent your new hire to meet everyone in the company who they might need to work with?

Try to think of creative ways to make new employees feel genuinely welcome. If you manage a restaurant, shouldn't every new employee be invited to bring a friend in for lunch? Not only will you make him feel more welcome, but it's also the perfect opportunity to give him a feel for the atmosphere and to demonstrate your standards of performance.

LET'S DO LUNCH

In any business, lunch is a great opportunity to make new people feel at home. At Barkley & Evergreen, on a new employee's first day, we assign a buddy to take him out to lunch. We don't want to take a chance that he might end up eating alone.

We also use the buddy system to make sure that each new employee is introduced to his coworkers and shown around the office. In general, he's there to make sure that everything goes smoothly. This buddy sticks close to him throughout his first month.

This might seem like it's a lot of trouble, but it works. The more welcome you make each employee feel, the less often you have to go through this process, because your turnover rate will go down. If you believe that your most important job is keeping your employees happy, then nothing should be more important to you than this.

You never get a second chance to make a first impression. It's true on the first date and it's just as true on the first day on the job. If you don't take the time to make each new employee's first day very special, you've stood him up.

WHEN IT'S TIME TO REHIRE YOUR STAFF

If you decide to change the culture of your company or department, you can make it a slow evolutionary process or you can try for something more dramatic. I prefer the dramatic approach.

It's relatively easy to indoctrinate new employees into a culture, but it's hard to get current employees used to a new system. They're used to the old ways, and most of them don't want to change.

When I decided to institute some new programs in our firm that were designed to help us do a better job of servicing clients, I wanted everyone in the company to start over. I wanted to rehire the entire staff.

We pretended that everyone was going to work for the company for the first time. To that end, we decided to have an orientation meeting for all the "new employees." On a Saturday morning at 8:00 AM, everyone assembled at a hotel for the big kickoff. In exchange for giving up half of their Saturday, everyone got an extra full day of vacation.

We talked about a new beginning. We talked about our new

goals, objectives, and standards of performance. We decided that we were going to send a signal to our clients of our renewed commitment to quality service. We told everyone that on Monday morning, they'd be working for a different company. In this case, it would have the same name, but a different personality.

In some ways, what we were presenting was unfair. We had changed the rules in the middle of the game. We told everyone that it was possible that some of them wouldn't like the new culture. In that event, we assured them that we'd do everything we could to help them find new jobs. For the rest, we offered new opportunities and new challenges. Finally, we took them through the same kind of orientation that we were going to give to new employees. In essence, we rehired everyone.

We started by letting them hear the talk I would be giving prospective new employees. Then, we gave them each a copy of our new company binder and a complete first-day orientation including the "pledge sheet" for everyone to sign. That's right—every single current employee had 30 days to revisit every other current employee at Barkley & Evergreen.

Lastly, we took them through the entire We Rent Helicopters® program. We had a new focus and a new slogan—and we wanted to be sure that everyone got the message. The mood that next Monday morning was upbeat. People could feel the change because we had brought it to their attention and focused on it.

If you manage a department or just a few people, you can still rehire your staff. Consult your people on what they think the goal should be. Maybe you can come up with a slogan that will summarize your vision. Most importantly, set aside a few hours when you can discuss the new beginning with all of your people.

If people gain a new enthusiasm about their work from the new culture, it might become the envy of the company—and start catching on.

If you're going to make a change, whether it's in a small department or a huge corporation, there's no point in dragging it out. Sports franchises know this. When a new coach comes in, he sets the team off in a new direction. He may even tell the players that they're going to have to win their positions all over again. Successful coaches and managers make the changes dramatically. Why? Because they've got to start winning RIGHT NOW.

Don't we all?

CONTINUING A GOOD THING

Since we had brought everyone together for that big orientation meeting, we decided to start a tradition by having an "annual meeting."

I can remember talking to a president of a company that had a large sales organization. "Business isn't looking good this year," he said. "We can't afford to hold our annual sales meeting. We'll save a lot of money if I just talk to the regional managers and filter the information down through them."

Now, there was a guy who knew how to squeak his company through tight times, right?

Personally, I thought he was nuts. And I told him so. If sales weren't good, they needed their annual sales meeting more than ever. They needed a pep talk.

It's a manager's job to pull everyone together and lead a cheer. Team spirit isn't built on a region-by-region basis; everyone in the organization has to feel it. You can't motivate the troops by talking to individuals.

A culture takes a minimum of five years to take root. It has to be nurtured in order to be healthy and prosper. That's why you need to renew it once a year at your annual meeting. You've got to fertilize and till the soil.

At Barkley & Evergreen, our entire staff gets together once a year for four hours on a Saturday morning. Everyone receives a full day off in exchange for their time. Our annual meeting is held "rain or shine." It's a great opportunity to emphasize the high points and reaffirm everything that is good about the company. If things aren't looking up (which fortunately isn't a theme that we have faced for a number of meetings), we offer honest solutions to problems. People are reassured and motivated after such a meeting.

To make sure that the meeting ends on a positive note, each person in the organization is brought up on the stage. Something positive about their past year's performance is told to the entire gathering. Then they're given their bonus check and their copy of the company yearbook.

WHEN THE GOING GETS TOUGH, THE TOUGH GET GOING

If a company or department hits hard times, there's a silver lining to the cloud. When people have their jobs at stake—when their personal economic survival is on the line—it's amazing how well they can work.

Don't get me wrong here. Bad times in a company ain't no picnic. But every problem offers an opportunity.

I spent a week with a group of executives at Harvard University Business School for a business seminar. At one of the marketing case study discussions, the professor described a company that had hit rock bottom. Its viability as a business entity was at stake. He asked us this question: "As president, would you be up-front with your people about the crisis?"

Most of the executives decided it would be wisest to stonewall the employees. They thought that people would be more productive if they believed everything were still peachy. This is a mistake.

People aren't stupid. If something's wrong, they sense it. And rumors fly. And if you're not honest about the situation, your people may get nervous and jump ship.

I was sitting at a business breakfast next to a company president whom I didn't know. Unable to think of anything to talk about, I told him that I was writing a book about motivating people and asked him how he went about motivating the people in his company. He said, "Oh, I don't have any trouble with that."

What?

This gentleman went on to explain that, until recently, his company had been in Chapter 11. The road that led to bankruptcy had been a long and tortuous one. They had just taken the company out of Chapter 11, and he thought that they were going to recover. He said that when people in an organization go through something like that, it's not very hard to keep them motivated and working as a team. His exact words were, "Survival is glue."

Many companies experience bad times. Rather than look at those times as trouble, recognize the opportunity to change your culture by getting everyone to pull together. By all means, don't circulate a memo giving the bad news. Call a big meeting and give everyone the facts face to face. Tell them how important they are to you and to your organization.

Don't be dismally sad either. You want to convey the point that you have confidence in your people, and that you will be giving 110 percent to hold the company together. Being honest with employees eliminates the need for water-cooler gossip. Your people will enjoy a new sense of family in the company, and they'll give you 110 percent in return.

When the crisis has passed, the seeds of a new culture will be in place. And, you can use that new environment as the basis upon which to build a successful organization.

A downturn in business is bad news. But, tough times can enable you to create one humdinger of a culture. Rally the troops behind your cause: economic survival. Build a team. Just remember to tell everybody that when the going gets tough, the tough get going.

Creating a brand-new corporate culture for your business or department is no easy task. It takes years to undo an unhealthy culture and get a good culture in your organization. If your company is a place where people don't enjoy their work, where rules are necessary for the most inane details, then it's probably time to change it.

- Corporate culture should replace company rules.

    It took God 40 days and 40 nights to flood the earth, but you've only got 30 days to indoctrinate new employees.

    When things get sticky, remember that survival can be the glue with which to build a new corporate culture.
- Everyone should have the responsibility to exceed his authority.

THOU SHALT NOT MIX BUSINESS AND PLEASURE

ONE OF THE BIGGEST problems with American business can be summed up in four words: thank God it's Friday. T.G.I.F. Americans work for the weekend. They work because they have to or because they want to make enough money to afford the luxuries in life. From the moment the alarm goes off on Monday morning, many people are already counting the hours to the weekend, the next vacation, or the next job. Few people admit to working because they want to.

I love my weekends as much as the next person, but I also love my weeks. My work is fun. And it's my belief that work should be fun for everybody. It doesn't make sense to spend five-sevenths of the week doing something you hate so that you can spend the other two-sevenths enjoying yourself.

When people truly enjoy their work, they're not only happier, but they also perform much better.

On May 25, 1965, Sonny Liston fought Cassius Clay for the Heavyweight Championship of the World. It seems incredible today, but Liston was an overwhelming favorite—something like nine to one.

A few days before the fight, Angelo Dundee, Cassius Clay's trainer, was interviewed about his fighter's chances. Of course, we wouldn't expect Angelo to predict anything other than Clay's victory. Indeed, he did predict that Clay would win decisively. But, the amazing thing was the reasoning behind his prediction.

Angelo did not tear down his opponent's boxing ability. He didn't even talk about Clay's superior skills. He predicted Clay's victory on the basis that he was having too much fun to lose. Angelo believed with his heart and soul that any fighter who was having that much fun preparing for a fight couldn't lose.

In case you're too young to remember the outcome, Angelo Dundee was right.

Unfortunately, not everyone is as self-inspired as Muhammad Ali was. That's why managers have to do some of the inspiring.

One such manager is Tommy Lasorda. In his first 12 seasons as manager of the Los Angeles Dodgers, he led his team to six Division Titles, four Pennants, and two World Series. Take a look at what Jonathan Rand, a sports columnist for the *Kansas City Star,* had to say about him after the Dodgers won the World Series in 1988.

"Tommy Lasorda does not have an 'off' switch. Some will tell you Lasorda's act gets old in a hurry. Many belittle his cheerleading, hugging, and sermons about the sanctity of Dodger blue. But nobody can make a good case that Lasorda's personal touch does not work.

"He credits the inspiration for his managing style to a can of condensed milk he spotted on his kitchen table when he was fifteen. It said: 'Contented cows give better milk' "

As Lasorda himself put it, "I am of the belief that contented people give better performances. I try to make it fun for them. I try to make them proud of the organization they represent."

As manager, it's your job to make work fun for your people. If you can do that, their performances will make you look good.

Most managers spend a lot of time trying to think of ways to increase productivity: systems for doing the work, increased division of labor, progress thermometers, etc. The easiest way to increase productivity is to make work fun. If the work is fun, people will want to do it. Not only that, but if people like doing their work, they'll do a better job.

Scott Bornstein, a friend of mine who is a psychologist and a memory specialist, taught me that people do better at things that they like. He preaches that making tasks fun makes them easier. In his speeches, he makes memory easy by making it into a game. He also encourages people to spread the gospel to their friends. In my seminars, I do just that.

I tell my audience that before I do anything, I'd like them to take a test. I explain that this test is very similar to an I.Q. test. It tests how much they can remember. And, furthermore, I tell them that their performance on this test will determine the approach I use in that seminar. Now that I've got them sweating, I ask them to take out a piece of paper and write down the numbers one to fifteen. I tell them that I'm going to give them a list of fifteen things and that they'll need to remember them in the order that I read them. Then I slowly give them the list. Number one is a blackboard; number two is a light switch; number three is the floor; and so on. Not surprisingly, no one ever remembers them all. Sometimes someone will get eleven or twelve, but never fifteen.

Then I reveal the reason I'm doing this exercise: to show them that if you make work fun, it immediately gets easier. When I said that they were taking a test, their stress levels went up. They got performance anxiety. When I read the list, I droned very methodically. I spoke in monotone. If people weren't so worried about how they were going to do, they might have started falling asleep.

After I explain everything, I go through the list with them again. This time I make it fun. I give them the mnemonic devices that Scott Bornstein developed, and it makes them laugh. For example, number one is a blackboard and they need to visualize it behind me. The blackboard is rectangular, green, and has a "1" in each of its four corners. Number two, the light switch, is easy to remember because a light switch has "2" positions—"on" and "off." The second time they do the exercise, they usually remember all fifteen objects correctly.

The point of this example is that memory isn't the only thing that improves when you decrease stress. Performance does too. When you make work fun for people—when you increase people's interest and decrease their stress level—they enjoy what they're doing. This causes them to perform better.

ARE YOU FUN TO BE AROUND?

You don't have to be a comedian to be fun to be around. You just
have to encourage people to enjoy what they're doing. You have to
be laid back enough to let the good times roll. That doesn't mean
that you should let people slack off on their work; it just means you
should help them to enjoy it. Many managers think that if they
encourage fun at work, they'll see productivity go out the window.
In fact, you should see a jump in productivity.

The best way to start making work fun is to make the work
environment more fun. Don't underestimate the importance of your
work environment. It can make or break morale in a company.

If you had to scrub floors with a toothbrush eight hours a day,
where would you rather do it—at Leavenworth maximum security
prison or at Disneyland? The task is the same, but environment
makes a heck of a difference.

That might be an extreme example, but there are offices out
there that approach the sterility and confinement of a prison. There
are lots of factors that take the fun out of your office. It could be
that your office is very political, and that people bicker and back-
stab. Or that there's more red tape and busy work than necessary.
The office could be overcrowded or, at the other extreme, people
could have little or no contact with other employees and therefore
feel isolated. Even the physical setup and design of the environment can put a damper on morale.

While there are many ways to make an office unbearably boring, there are even more ways to cheer things up. If you don't know
how to start, give your work environment a careful look. Maybe
the place looks dull. You can start by giving the walls a coat of a
different color paint or reorganizing the office to make it more
comfortable. It could even be as simple as raising some blinds to let
the sunshine in.

It's amazing to me how many companies have very strict rules
about what people can put up on their office walls. Many companies won't allow anything. These company policies restrict ev-

eryone's ability to extend his personality to his work area, and such rules make for a very boring environment.

More important than changing the physical structure of the office, you should do some fun things at work. We do quite a few extra things at Barkley & Evergreen to keep the fun factor high.

For starters, we have an employee newsletter. I was once a big deal newspaper publisher—I started a class newspaper in the sixth grade. I didn't know how to type, so I hand-wrote the whole thing. Then, since that was the pre-copy machine era, I simply circulated it around the class. The paper died after one issue due to writer's cramp.

I think every company should have an employee newsletter. Its circulation should be restricted to employees. If you want to communicate to your customers as well, don't try to kill two birds with one stone. You'll just kill a good idea.

In my business, there's a thing called "production values." That's a fancy way of describing how "slick" something is. If you spend a lot of money on a brochure, it should have good production values. Expensive network television commercials usually have good production values, too. But, when it comes to your company newsletter, less is more.

Run it off on a copy machine or take it to a quick print shop. Even if you only manage three people, it's still worth your while to put together a newsletter. You may only have the resources to type a one-page paper each month, but it'll still be fun and appreciated.

Don't try to make it slick. You don't want it to look like propaganda from above. The slicker it is, the less it will be read. A good rule of thumb is: the hokier, the better.

Find someone in your company or department who wants to be the editor, and encourage everyone else to submit material. You shouldn't be looking for professional journalists. In fact, the paper will probably be more fun to read if it isn't professionally written. Remember, we're talking to our family.

And what are we telling them? All the news that's fit to print and a lot of news that isn't.

I prefer an editor who's got a little *National Enquirer* streak in him. People in our office are pretty careful about what they say in front of our newsletter editor because they may find it in print in the next month's issue. In addition to dirty laundry, we include announcements of new employees, employee promotions, anniversaries, birthdays, and all the other life-cycle stuff. But, we also have employee profiles that frequently fall short of being flattering—all in fun, of course.

I have found over the years that I seem to unknowingly provide some pretty juicy material. Any mistake I make and any little quirk I have, no matter how small, seems to find its way into our newsletter.

Every year, when our summer interns get ready to return to college for their senior year, many request to be put on a mailing list for our monthly newsletter. With all the things college students have to read, that's quite a compliment.

We recently began a new tradition at Barkley & Evergreen. One day, I was looking through a list of suggestions that our employees had turned in when one of them jumped off the page. Our traffic manager suggested that we produce a company yearbook. I was so excited about that idea that I immediately sought her out. I told her that if she would be in charge of photography, we'd do it.

These days, you'll find our yearbook editor, camera in hand, at all our company events, from staff meetings to the annual picnic. Toward the end of the year, we pass out ballots for different categories like best looking, worst dressed, most likely to be late for work, etc. The pictures highlighting the year and the results of the balloting are printed and distributed at the Christmas party.

If you'd like a copy, write us. If you'd like a copy of the pictures we decided not to use, I'm sorry to report that they are unavailable at any price.

If you or someone in your company has a video camera, I've got another idea for you: make company home movies. We have a lot of fun at our company picnic. But, we have almost as much fun in the dead of winter when we watch the videotape of the company picnic. We all gather in the conference room at lunch to relive the absurd behavior that some of our staff exhibited six months earlier.

We also take the camera to the annual Christmas party, the company softball games, and anything else we can think of. At a staff meeting later on, we haul out a tape and play it for everyone. We usually have to do a little editing and we frequently add a musical track just to make it more interesting.

Our office manager is our cinematographer. He's no Steven Spielberg. In fact, at one Christmas party, he was walking around with a drink in one hand and the camera in the other. I guess that wasn't his first drink, because he didn't realize the camera was on. If you send your name, address, and a check for $25, we'll send you 20 minutes of videotape of the ceiling in the Allis Plaza Hotel.

While we're on the subject of the Christmas party, I've got a suggestion that can make it a lot more fun. Do you hire a band for your office Christmas party? If so, this is your chance to give some employees their fifteen minutes of fame. Make arrangements with the band ahead of time so that you can strike up the company band while they're on break.

In any organization, there have got to be some people who play musical instruments. If there aren't any in your organization, there's still hope: a cappella is back in.

I wouldn't want to put our band up against a professional one for musical ability. Sometimes they play and sing a little off-key. But I will put them up against any band for enthusiasm and fun. Isn't that what the Christmas party is all about?

If you hire a disc jockey, I'm sure you've got people who have always wanted to spin discs. All you have to do is find them.

Depending on what kind of business you're in, you can devise all sorts of ways to give the troops a boost. And you don't necessarily have to be subtle. For example, new business is the lifeblood of an advertising agency. When we get some, we like to make a big deal out of it. I immediately go to our board room and take the "New Business Cymbals" off the wall. Then I go to the reception area and crash them hard enough to set off the San Andreas fault. I march through the office, periodically banging the cymbals in case somebody didn't hear the first time. People stop working, grab their company kazoos, and get in line. (What? Don't you have company kazoos?) We march together, cymbals and kazoos playing, to the board room.

Waiting in the board room is champagne. I announce the new business and give a brief background on how we got it. Then we have a toast, or two.

Later, we paint the name and logo of our new client on one of the cymbals. When the cymbals are full of names—and they nearly are—we'll buy a new pair.

I told a friend of mine about our new tradition. He looked at me like I should be locked up and said, "Only you could think of something like that." Actually, I didn't come up with this idea; one of my employees did. And, to be honest with you, there are no statistics out there on the effects of playing percussion instruments on employee productivity. But we have fun.

I'd like to point out that if your employees would feel comfortable giving you a suggestion like crashing cymbals when you get new business, you know you've succeeded in creating an open office environment.

Doing fun things at work is only the first step in making your work environment enjoyable. You've already learned what it takes to help people enjoy being at work. Now, you have to concentrate on making people enjoy working.

I feel very lucky. I love what I do. I think marketing and advertising are extremely interesting. And I love people. Unfortunately, not everyone is as happy as I am.

In Utopia, the way to make work fun is to find everyone a job that they love. Since my kids live in Utopia, I've encouraged each of them to pursue careers that they can enjoy. I'm confident that if they try hard enough, they'll find just the right jobs for themselves. Although, if my youngest son's interests don't change, he may have trouble finding his ideal job. No one wants to hire a guy to play video games.

It would be ideal if everyone you hired absolutely loved his work. Unfortunately, that's not the case. So it's your job to help your people become more enthusiastic about their work.

How to Throw a Good Meeting

Every manager should spend some time with all the people he manages. This is your chance to demonstrate your enthusiasm for your work and hope that a little will rub off. If you're fortunate enough to work closely with all of your people, you've got plenty of opportunities to show your enthusiasm. As president, I manage a lot of people. I have very few opportunities to work with all of my staff. So I take advantage of the chances that I get.

Every business has meetings. And most people dread them, and with good cause: they're usually boring. Not only that, but meetings interrupt people's work. I'm not a big advocate of having lots of meetings.

However, regardless of what business you're in, there's one meeting that is always worth interrupting work for: the monthly staff meeting. This is the manager's chance to keep employee morale high and to make sure that everybody's singing from the same sheet of music. But most importantly, it should be fun.

Ideally, this should be a meeting of all the people in the company, but if that's not possible you can certainly have one for everyone in your department. Those of you who already have to attend several meetings a week might not see the need for this extra meeting. But, consider those people on your staff who don't attend regular meetings. You all need to get together once a month to remind yourselves that you're on the same team.

If you're the president of the company, try to have a meeting with everyone at least once per month. Don't be discouraged if your company is located in several different cities. It can be done. I know the president of a company that has offices in four cities, and he personally conducts the staff meetings in all four locations.

Monthly staff meetings don't have to take more than 30 or 40 minutes. You'd be amazed at how much you can cover in a short period of time. In fact, the more you cover, the faster the pace of the meeting, and the more fun everybody will have.

I asked several managers who observe this ritual to share with me the kinds of things they cover in their monthly meetings. I've put these together with a composite of some of our agenda items to give you some idea of what to cover:

- Introduce new employees.
- Award gifts to people who are celebrating their anniversary with the company that month.
- Give birthday gifts to people who have birthdays that month.
- Show-and-tell new work that the company has done, or talk about new business that's been gained.
- Announce any employee promotions. (In our company, that means we give them the framed revised business card.)
- Call for committee reports from the chairpersons of the various committees (party committees, in particular).
- Review a particular company policy that isn't being followed or has changed. It's so much better to talk about it than to send out a memo.
- Present the Employee-of-the-Month Award.
- Share a success story from a department or employee.
- Read any complimentary letters or notes that have come in from customers.
- Distribute the company newsletter.
- Report on the status of suggestions.
- Use your imagination. I enjoy being in front of an audience. (I do a five-minute routine when the light in the refrigerator comes on.) So I really look forward to these meetings, and I try hard to make them entertaining. In fact, some people have described our monthly staff meetings as 50 percent pep rally. You wouldn't get an argument from me.

Some time back, a woman at our company had to go into the hospital for major surgery. She was off work for almost two months. I was talking to her on the phone one day when she mentioned that she was really going to miss our next staff meeting.

So when I entered the room for that month's staff meeting, I wore a surgical gown and mask, and had a stethoscope around my neck. With a video camera running for the entire meeting, I conducted the proceedings donned in hospital garb. At the end of the meeting, we went around the room and everybody wished her a speedy recovery. Then we sent the tape to her home so she'd have something to watch besides "As the World Turns."

She called me the next day to tell me that it was the nicest get-well gift she had received. And we all had a lot of fun giving it to her.

On another occasion, one of my employees let me in on some real dirt. She had been at church the previous Sunday when she saw our creative director parade up to the front in a Boy Scout uniform, followed by a line of nine-year-old Cub Scouts. She was unable to control her laughter. Of all the images one could conjure up of our creative director, Cub Scout Leader is definitely not one of them. That gave me an idea.

I ran to his office and asked him if he would conduct our next staff meeting dressed in his Boy Scout regalia. He didn't think my idea was nearly as funny as I did, but I finally persuaded him that everyone would enjoy the fun at his expense. When the day arrived, he came into my office before the meeting and, with the door locked, changed into his uniform.

There's not a bartender in Kansas City who would have believed it.

After everyone had assembled, he walked into the room. It took five minutes for the laughter to die down. In fact, he finally got everyone's attention by putting up two fingers, the Scout sign that means it's time to quiet down.

New employees often come up after a meeting to tell me that their previous employer never had meetings like ours. They can't believe all the fun they've been missing.

My son Dan spent the summer between high school and his first year of college working in our office. As with most teenagers, a summer job wasn't his idea of fun; it was an economic necessity. He stopped working a week before he was to leave for college. But, before he left the office on his last day, he stopped by to see if I'd mind if he came in the next Wednesday morning to attend the staff meeting. It was so much fun that he didn't want to miss it.

Make your monthly staff meetings fun, and your people won't want to miss them. In a fun atmosphere, even the serious issues become more palatable. When people are having fun they're more creative, open, and communicative—the essentials of a good meeting.

Always begin and end on a good note, and try to come up with a surprise—no matter how small—for each meeting. If you put a lot of effort into these meetings, people will learn to look forward to them, and so will you.

YOUR OFFICE SHOULDN'T END AT THE FRONT DOOR

Once you've succeeded in getting everyone in a good mood at your monthly staff meeting, you have to maintain that spirit by making the individual jobs more fulfilling. If you want people to share your excitement about their work, you've got to do everything you can to keep their jobs exciting and fun.

There is probably not one person in your organization whose job encompasses all aspects of your product or service. Most people are responsible for just one part of your finished product. The people in accounting or the mail room may not ever have anything to do with your product or service. In fact, your entire company may be responsible for just one link in a large chain that makes up a service. For example, some high technology firms produce just a few complicated parts of a large machine. They may design the tubing for a particular engine and never have anything to do with the rest of the engine.

Because of this division of labor, employees may fail to understand why the role they're playing is important. People are so busy concentrating on their tasks that they have trouble seeing the bigger picture. That's how they become bored and frustrated with their work.

This is where you come in. It's the manager's job to take the horse blinders off of people. One of the best ways to broaden an employee's perspective is to send him out on a field trip. Whether it's to one of your suppliers, to a client's operation, or to another department in your company, a field trip is a great learning experience. Field trips are not just educational; they also help employees to see their jobs from a fresh point of view.

Consider the benefits of having everyone on your staff put in some time in the field. If you're a lawyer, every "nonprofessional" in your office should see a trial at least once a year. If legal aides understand the importance of their research—that the outcome of trials can depend on it—they may work harder.

If you're a CPA, your secretaries should occasionally go out into the field and help take an inventory. They might learn something that they can apply to their own jobs or understand the significance of some of the things they have to do.

A field trip doesn't necessarily entail going very far. Sometimes, there's an opportunity to gain a new perspective right in the next room. For example, a friend of mine is director of training for a large national restaurant chain. He told me that he instructs his restaurant managers to bring both the chef and the dishwasher out into the restaurant so they can get a feel for the business.

The chef made sense to me. After all, it adds a little charm to a guest's experience when the chef visits the dining room. But the dishwasher? My friend explained that if you were a dishwasher, and you never had a chance to be in the front of the restaurant, you might begin to believe that a pancake was something you used to put out a cigarette. So my friend has his dishwashers work an occasional shift busing tables. This gives them a chance to see customers enjoying those pancakes, and gives them a different perspective on how important it is to get the dishes, glasses, and silverware clean.

There's another type of field trip which can be beneficial to your employees. Every now and then, people need to go out and meet the people on the other end of their telephone lines.

Let's take your chief financial officer. Normally, you wouldn't think that he would have a need to interact directly with the customers. But, if you ever run into a collection problem or have a discrepancy with a bill, it certainly helps when the two people on the phone have met.

You can't meet everybody you talk to. But you never know when the opportunity will present itself. For example, Bill Lenahan is the president of Sears Business Centers, and is also a client of mine. When my secretary was on vacation in Chicago, she decided to stop by and visit his secretary. She had spoken with her on the phone countless times and decided it would be a good idea to meet her in person. It has made their phone relationship a lot more friendly and productive.

If you're truly committed to providing outstanding service for your customers, everybody in the company needs to take a field trip once in a while. It will put the business and their respective jobs in a fresh perspective. But more importantly, it'll help make everyone's job a lot more fun.

"LEADERSHIP AND LEARNING ARE INDISPENSABLE
TO EACH OTHER."   —*John F. Kennedy*

The reason why field trips are so effective is that people love to learn. Even if we were happy to finish school so that we could get started on our real lives, few of us want to stop learning. When employees find themselves stuck in a rut—when they deal with the same information day after day—they get antsy. No one wants to stick around in a job that never changes.

If you want to help people stay enthusiastic about their work, you've got to make sure that they keep learning.

About ten years ago, our company was going through tremendous turmoil. We were losing employees so fast that our clients needed a scorecard to keep track of who was working on their accounts.

Unable to figure out why people didn't want to continue to work for a company that had what I modestly considered to be inspired leadership, I hired a consultant to help me find the answer. We decided that he should hold confidential interviews with everyone in the office.

While he was conducting these interviews, I began to doubt whether he was going to get the information that I really needed. The people who were still at Barkley & Evergreen were probably pretty happy with their jobs; otherwise they'd be gone, too. The people whom he really needed to interview were the ones who had already left. I gave him a list of the people who had recently flown the coop and told him to try and get interviews with them, too.

Several days later, he met with me to give me his report and recommendations. He started out by telling me that most of the people thought our company was a really nice place to work. (Much to my chagrin, they thought I was OK but not inspiring.) The problem was that most people viewed our company as a stopping off point in their careers, not the place where they'd ultimately end up. The length of their stay was not based on the speed of their advancement or their compensation. They stayed until they'd learned everything we could teach them about the business. Then they left. As my consultant put it, "They're sucking you dry and moving on."

Solving the problem was not simple. We set out to create an environment in which people would learn so much that they wouldn't want to leave. What we ended up with was a four-pronged program that focuses on personal growth.

This program was (and continues to be) so successful that I now recommend it to all of our clients who are trying to decrease turnover. Our employee education program is as follows:

1. *Job-related*—This is professional training. Most of the courses are taught within each department by the department head. They focus on job skills. These courses teach employees little tricks of the trade and some of the skills necessary for a promotion. Most of the companies which do offer employee education programs stop with this type of training.

2. *Industry-related*—These courses help our people understand the different aspects of the advertising industry. Often it's as simple as having each department head speak to the other depart-

ments. For example, our creative director might explain layout design to our account executives. Not only do the account executives learn something about making an ad, but they're also better prepared to present creative work to clients.

3. *General business*—These are my personal favorites. General business classes are taught in our "Lunch 'n' Learn" program. People have the option to come during lunch hour. We provide the pizza and soft drinks. These classes cover a variety of business subjects, from writing a terrific letter to reading a financial statement. And, for the people interested in hard-core business education, we do Harvard case studies.

4. *Personal growth*—These courses include subjects like tax planning and buying a house. But as the title suggests, they also include everything from pottery to the history of rock 'n' roll. Some of the courses that we've offered are:

- Tips on Using a 10-Key Adding Machine
- How to Get the Most Out of the Public Library
- How to Win at the Horse Races
- Criticism and Discipline Skills
- Tips on Conducting Interviews
- Presentation Skills

It's easy to get experts outside your company to come in and conduct these classes free of charge. My stockbroker jumped at the offer to let him explain the stock market to a group of eager listeners. And real estate and insurance agents will all but pay you for the opportunity to come and give an informational talk. It's great exposure for them and their companies. Usually we can find someone to come in and give a talk for free. But, if enough people ask for a course, we offer it whether we have to pay for it or not.

Sometimes an employee at Barkley & Evergreen wants to teach a class. These are some of the best-attended classes that we offer. Some of your most interesting speakers might be right in front of your face. All they need is the forum in which to do it.

If you have a very small staff, you can modify this program to suit you. Maybe you can send away for copies of pertinent journal articles or books and lead an occasional discussion group, rather than holding actual classes. Instead of bringing speakers in, you could take your group out to seminars and speeches.

The difference between corporate education programs and traditional school is that in corporate education, the students aren't graded; the teachers and the classes are. A good education program is considered a job benefit. Not only can it help retain people, but it can also be an effective tool in recruiting.

Recently, we were trying to recruit a young man for our account service department. The head of the department came to me to see if I would talk with this prospective employee, because we hadn't been able to get him to make a decision.

When we met, the young man explained that he had another offer at a higher position and a higher salary. So he asked me why he should take the job with our firm instead of accepting the other offer.

I told him that his decision hinged on where he felt he was in his career. Then I took him through our training program in great detail. I also gave him copies of the current Harvard case studies that we were working on. I showed him a list of the upcoming classes—both the required ones and the optional lunch and after-work sessions. Then I told him that he would have to decide which was more important to him: the higher position and salary, or the education.

A week later, he accepted the position with our firm. He opted for the education. What's more, he wanted to know if he could have some of the course materials in advance so that he could be caught up with everyone else when he attended his first class.

GET SPECIFIC

I can tell you how to make your work environment more enjoyable, how to make meetings more lively, and how to put interesting programs in your department. These are all aspects of work that most every manager can relate to. But, I can't tell you how to make the particular jobs in your department more fun. Only you have the knowledge and experience to do that. Talk to your employees, and see what they think will make their jobs more fun. Be open to suggestions, and be willing to take a risk with your new program.

Western Auto's new corporate culture program includes a productivity game. Western Auto wanted to make work more fun for the cashiers, mechanics, and specialists at their many stores. They also wanted to recognize excellence in specific job skills. We came up with the Western Auto 1990 Olympics.

The Western Auto Olympics is similar to the traditional Olympics, except there's a twist. The events in the Western Auto Olympics are all work-related. The events include tasks that are in people's job descriptions: like ringing up a sale, changing a tire, or finding an item in the store. People who win at their own stores go on to districts, regionals, and ultimately national competition.

The prizes for the Western Auto Olympics include recognition, awards, and travel vacation packages.

If someone wants to practice for the Western Auto Olympics, they have forty hours every week in which to do it. Now, when there's a line of customers at the parts counter, it's no longer a problem but an opportunity to practice.

Participation is voluntary. Even so, almost three-fourths of their employees decided to play. They had nothing to lose. The games themselves were a lot of fun, the prizes were appealing, and the competition ensured that people who take their work seriously would be recognized. What more could you ask for?

A similar program may work for you. You'll most certainly need to adapt it to suit your particular type of business. And if this type of program won't work for you, you'll need to use your imagination to devise your own program.

Will productivity shoot up immediately after your program begins? Who knows? Maybe you won't find the perfect program the first time around. But, if you've succeeded even slightly in making people's jobs more exciting, you've accomplished something. In addition, taking an interest in people and trying to make their work more fun sends them the message that their happiness is important to you. Your employees will appreciate it. The bottom line is that if you want to increase productivity, you should make it your top priority to ensure that people enjoy their work.

ARE WE HAVING FUN YET?

If the people in your organization are having fun, I'll guarantee you that the business is doing well. In fact, if they're having more fun than they've ever had, you're probably in the midst of a record year.

When you walk through your office to see how everyone's doing, the last thing you want to ask people is "How are you doing?" You'll just get reflex responses. No one thinks about that question before he answers. When I walk through my office, I ask people if they're having fun. That's a question that won't result in a conditioned response. And, I really find out if they're having a good time. If they're not, I know I've got a problem.

One time, I was conducting one of my seminars when an executive asked me about my aversion to financial statements. I told him that I can tell more about how a company's doing by asking everyone if they're having fun than I can by pouring over financial statements.

He found my remark a little incredible. So, I assured him that I always ask the chief financial officer if he's having fun, too. After all, my mama didn't raise a fool.

WHO NEEDS AN EXCUSE FOR A PARTY?

The last, and certainly most obvious, way to foster fun times is to have parties. But, there's a reason why this suggestion is last: parties can't be the only thing you do. Many companies throw parties, and they turn out just like the office—cold and boring. If your office isn't a fun place to work, then your people won't want to celebrate.

On the other hand, if your coworkers are like family, and they have fun at work, then having company parties will be second nature. Like all of these suggestions, you can't go out and throw the best party the first time you try. Some people will feel uncomfortable with it. That's why it's especially important to consult your employees before you arrange anything. Nobody appreciates mandatory fun.

Once you've fostered a fun environment, your people will want to get together after work. When this is the case, you shouldn't have to have an excuse for a party. But, I've included some excuses, nonetheless.

The company sports team is a reliable old stand-by. Most companies sponsor a softball or bowling team, but there are a lot more opportunities than that. How about an indoor soccer team or a monthly golf and tennis tournament?

Barkley & Evergreen sponsored a company decathlon. We formed a decathlon committee, which met a few times after work and put the whole thing together. We had two teams, which were divided equally by sex—male and female—not those who do and those who don't.

Since we don't have a lot of pole vaulters, the committee needed to come up with a list of feasible events. Some of us, particularly yours truly, were looking for less strenuous activities like duplicate bridge or chess. Fortunately, I was overruled. The events were:

- bowling
- basketball free throws
- golf
- 100-meter free-style swimming
- 100-yard dash
- one-mile run
- miniature golf (my personal favorite)
- horseshoes
- pitching pennies against a wall (for our ex-New Yorkers)
- singles tennis tournament

Each month, one of the events would be held either on a weekend or after work. Points were awarded for each event. The individual event winners and the overall winning team won trophies and our company's traditional prize—extra days off. In fact, extra days off has become part of our culture. Your own decathlon can do wonders for the team spirit in your company or department.

When it comes to company outings, we don't take a back seat to anybody. In fact, we have so many outings that the charter bus drivers are getting to know our names.

Every function has its own committee, which is given a budget and the responsibility of making sure that this year's event is the best in the company's history.

Take the company picnic, for example. We try to dream up all kinds of events—some individual and some team sports. Winners get extra days off. The picnic is held on a regular work day with only a temporary switchboard operator back at the office. The cost to the company is minimal when you consider what happens to morale.

We also have family outings, like company night at the Kansas City Royals and a tailgate party for a Kansas City Chiefs game. The challenge for the committees is to do just a bit more than other companies do. If we can get players to give autographs to the kids after the game, we do it. (Some of the "kids" have beards.)

As if that weren't already enough fun and games, we come up with all kinds of reasons to have more parties. In fact, every single person in the company has the authority to come up with an excuse for a party. Of course, these parties are dutch treat, since there's a limit to how much we can budget for parties.

If you're going to develop team spirit, you can't have employee relationships that end at 5:00 PM. If your business is just a job to your employees, they'll never be willing to go the extra mile. For that reason, you need to find any excuse you can to have after-work activities and parties.

Some of the excuses for throwing a party get pretty creative. The morning the machinists' union went out on strike at Eastern Airlines, I got a memo explaining that there would be a sympathy strike by our employees. All work was to stop at 5:30 PM Friday (a half hour after our official closing time, mind you) and the "sympathy strikers" were to assemble for a rally. This rally was held at a local watering hole. Everyone was encouraged to bring their own picket signs.

I'll never forget the day that a fly got into one of the offices in our creative department. After the fly was exterminated, a memo was circulated, explaining that there would be a wake that evening at the home of the individual who killed it. When I arrived, the fly lay in state in a match box on the dining room table. After a very brief service, appetizers and beverages were served.

Occasionally, we invite employees of competitive firms to some of our impromptu parties. It's great for recruiting. They see how much fun we have and want to be a part of it. In fact, one of our senior creative people was recruited to our company in just that manner. Before he came on board, however, we made sure he knew that he'd be working his tail off in between parties.

Last, but not least, we use the old weather excuse. When spring arrives, we get outside at least once a month for a pot luck lunch in the parking lot. The company provides the hot dogs, hamburgers, and soft drinks, and everybody brings a side dish or dessert. We eat, visit, and play a little parking lot Frisbee. When we go back to work, we're all refreshed and feel a whole lot better about the place at which we've chosen to spend a big part of our lives.

That's about all the excuses I can think of. If you need any more, talk to a teenager.

- "Contented cows give better milk." —Pet Milk
- "Leadership and learning are indispensable to each other." — John F. Kennedy

THOU SHALT LABOR FOR THY BOSS

ONE OF THE GOALS I had when I graduated from Northwestern University in 1964 was to end up working for myself. I thought that "self-employed" was the best possible position anyone could be in. As far as I was concerned, I didn't ever want to work for anyone else. I wanted the freedom to be my own boss.

But it didn't take me long to realize that reality was 180 degrees from what I thought when I was just starting my business career. Some presidents are responsible to shareholders; some presidents are the shareholders; but, all presidents have certain constituencies in common. Regardless of who owns the company, the president has the ultimate responsibility for the welfare of the employees, their families, the company's suppliers and their families, and the customers. Loading all of that responsibility onto anyone's shoulders will certainly eliminate any feeling of freedom.

I can still remember when my fledgling company had its first company picnic that was attended by all the employees and their families. It was downright scary to look around and realize how many people were counting on me to make the right decisions.

However, the anxiety that I experienced as president of my company at that company picnic was probably not much different than what I would have experienced had I been there as a department head responsible for a group of employees. Or, for that matter, I'm sure the employees who were there with their children could have verbalized similar feelings.

WHO ARE YOU REALLY WORKING FOR?

Everyone is really self-employed. Regardless of the title you have on your business card, ultimately you are responsible for yourself and to yourself. What does all of this really mean? For one thing, it means that you are responsible for the timeliness and quality of the work you do. It also means that you're responsible for your own career. The person that drives you has to be you.

This point is best illustrated by one of my favorite advertising stories. A young copywriter had just started his career with a large advertising agency. The creative director of the agency gave the new copywriter his first assignment with the direction to leave the finished work with the department secretary when he was done. Several days after completing the assignment the copywriter still hadn't heard any feedback. So, he went to the creative director's office and asked him what he thought of the copy. The creative director asked if that was the best job the copywriter could do. The copywriter said, "No," and proceeded to take back the work so that he could give it another shot.

Two days later the copywriter dropped off the revised work with the creative director's secretary and waited for a response. When a week had passed and the copywriter still hadn't heard anything, he again approached his boss and asked him what he thought of the work. Once again, the creative director simply asked if the copy was the best work that the young copywriter could do.

The copywriter said that he'd like to give it one more shot and took back his work. One week later the copywriter walked into the creative director's office with the final revision of the copy. He explained to his manager that he had reworked this assignment over and over until he was absolutely positive that this was the best he could do. With that, the creative director informed the copywriter that he would now take the time to read what had been written.

Don't wait for someone else to demand the best of you. Demand it of yourself. That's what it really means to be self-employed. You are responsible for your own career and the quality of your own work. You don't work for a company. You work for your family, your friends, your coworkers, and most importantly, yourself.

IT TAKES A TOUGH MAN TO MAKE A TENDER CHICKEN

If you're going to demand the best of yourself, you can't possibly settle for other people's standards. It's more important that you set and meet your own standards than try to meet someone else's. Frank Perdue owned a poultry company in Maryland. When he started his business, he could have been content following the government's standards that regulate the quality of chickens sold in the United States. But, Frank Perdue had his own standards, and they were a lot higher than Uncle Sam's. Today, Frank's company sells more chickens than any other company in the Northeast.

You should never be content to do what is required of you by others. If you want your work to stand out as exceptional, you have to have higher standards for yourself than anyone else has for you. That's the key to being self-employed. It's much easier to follow someone else's guidelines than it is to set your own. But, remember that you can't stand out by being a sheep.

CONTROLLING THE CLOCK

Whether you're the CEO of a Fortune 500 company or an entry-level employee of a small firm, there's one thing that we all have in common—we've each got only 24 hours a day to do with what we want. As any basketball player will tell you, the most powerful person in the game is the one who is controlling the clock. Part of being self-employed is understanding that you control the clock. If you're really self-employed, there's nobody to watch the clock for you. You don't have people telling you what to do and when. That's why it's important to be in control of how you spend your time.

The popular solution to time management problems is to buy a daily planner. But, daily planners don't tell you what you did on a given day. They only tell you what you planned to do. The only way to know what you did is to write it down. Keep a time sheet.

In order to become more efficient, you have to check your progress. Can you imagine a marathon runner who didn't know how fast he could run a mile, or whether he ran faster at the start or finish of a race? In order to improve at something, you have to know how you're doing and what you need to change.

To know how efficiently you're really working, you have to keep a personal time sheet. This time sheet is a record of what you actually did. It's not for anyone but yourself to see, so you can be honest. It's not intended to make you put your nose to the grindstone until you end up with a snout. It's a way for you to find out how you're spending (and wasting) your time.

It only takes about ten or fifteen minutes a day to do. You can get an idea of how you're doing by keeping a time sheet for just a week. If you want to check your progress, pick it back up again later.

First come up with a list of the types of functions and responsibilities you have. For example, your list could include the following: personnel problems, customer contact, new business development, general administrative work, internal meetings, financial planning and review, developing a positive corporate culture, etc. Don't forget to have one item on your list called "coffee breaks/rest room breaks." They tend to go together.

Estimate in advance what percentage of your time you want to spend in each category. Then, create a daily chart and divide it into 30-minute increments. I'm ambitious; the one I keep for myself is in 15-minute increments. Make each of the items on your list a column heading. Each day, put a check mark under the appropriate column for each half-hour you've spent on that category.

Each week, add the total number of check marks. That becomes your common denominator. Now add the check marks under your first heading and make that the numerator. Doing the long division will tell you what percentage of your time you spent on that item. Do that for each item.

IT'S TIME FOR CONFESSION

Make sure you devote one column to "miscellaneous time." I don't think I'm the Lone Ranger when it comes to having a certain amount of each day in which I don't get anything specific done. Everyone needs to have some free time every day just to take a deep breath and reflect on where they've been and where they're going—call it a kind of mental-health break. Before you start this exercise, estimate the percentage of miscellaneous time along with your other estimates.

At the end of the week, if you're dissatisfied with the discrepancy between the time you planned to spend and the time you actually spent on each of your responsibilities, you can reallocate your time. You might find that there are more efficient ways to work.

Don't decide that you can't do a time sheet because you have too much other work to do. Give it a shot. If time is money, it follows that you've got to invest a little bit if you want to make any.

"SOME DAYS YOU'RE A BUG AND SOME DAYS YOU'RE A WINDSHIELD."

About six years ago, on a Monday afternoon, I called my attorney and close friend Leonard Rose to tell him about a big new client we had just landed. I told him that this was just another example of how good our company was and what a great profession I had chosen.

On Wednesday morning, I called Leonard because we had just lost a large client and I was plenty worried. As I recall, I felt my options ranged from slitting my wrists to jumping off the roof of the building.

On Friday evening, Leonard and I went out to celebrate another new account Barkley & Evergreen had just nailed down—our biggest account ever. It was just as we were preparing to toast the victory that Leonard came forth with his memorable quote, "Some days you're a bug and some days you're a windshield."

Business is an emotional roller coaster. When things are going great and your company just landed a new piece of business, everyone is sky high. When your biggest customer leaves for a competitor, everyone in the organization is ready to hold a wake.

People who think of themselves as self-employed stay off of emotional roller coasters.

When everything appears great, don't let yourself float away on the clouds. Things are never as good as they seem. When it looks as if things couldn't possibly be worse, it's time for you to pump yourself up and get to work. The best time to show people what you're really made of is when everyone else is hanging their heads in defeat.

Imagine the following scenario. There are 14 seconds left in a basketball game. The other team just took the lead for the first time in the game, 77–76. Our coach calls a time out. The players walk angrily toward the bench. It's the coach's job to slap every one of their butts and get them psyched up about the upcoming play. The team runs a picture-perfect play and scores. Time out again. The players are jumping up and down. Does the coach congratulate them? No way. He yells at them to calm down and get their heads back in the game. He brings them back down to earth. It's his job to maintain the team's emotional equilibrium.

But you don't have to be the coach in order to assume a position of leadership. Several years ago, our company was going through some real tough times. I was trying hard to keep morale up, but it wasn't easy. Even I was depressed. One morning, one of our copywriters came into my office to tell me that he wanted me to know that I could count on him and to reassure me that things were definitely going to get better. He took the opportunity to get my head back into the game. When he did, my opinion of him as a potential leader changed a lot.

SELF-EMPLOYED IS A STATE OF MIND

Rabbi Dr. Leo Beck, leader of the Jewish community in Hitler's Germany, said: "More important than any sermon the rabbi gives is the sermon the rabbi is."

If your goal is to be self-employed, the first thing you've got to realize is that you already are. All of us are self-employed. In fact, all of us are managers—even if we're currently only managing ourselves. The important thing to remember is that we must be able to visualize ourselves in that capacity before we can ever possibly accomplish it.

I love golf. I'm not very good at it, but when it comes to enthusiasm I'm a scratch player. Any really good golfer will tell you that you can't possibly hit a good shot until you can visualize it. As a matter of fact, if the picture you have in your mind is that you're going to hit the ball out-of-bounds, you probably will.

Start picturing yourself as self-employed. Start visualizing what you want to do with the rest of your business career. Then, start making your vision a reality.

- Self-employed is a state of mind.
- Satisfying the boss is second only to satisfying yourself.
- Managers shouldn't ride roller coasters.

CONCLUSION

IN ADVERTISING, the only thing harder to write than a 60-second commercial is a 30-second commercial. And, the only thing harder to write than a 30-second commercial is a 10-second commercial. The less time or space for your message, the more difficult the task to communicate.

So, I now step up to the task of writing a conclusion to this book. Somehow, shortly and sweetly, I want to give you a synopsis of what it's all about.

The easiest way for me to do that, based upon my professional background, is to put it in marketing terms. There certainly hasn't been a shortage of books, many of them well done, that deal with marketing to consumers and trade customers. However, if our companies are going to survive into the next century, we all better start thinking about how we are going to market to the most important audience we have to reach—the people we work with.

The steps to marketing to this most important group are simple. They are no different than marketing to anyone else. I have dealt with a lot of people who had the title of marketing manager. I believe that every manager has a marketing function and responsibility to focus on the needs of the people they work with.

First, we have to understand what our "customer" really wants, and then we have to deliver it to them. My experience has been that my most important "customers"—the people I work with—want responsibility, recognition, education, opportunity, and love. My job is to see that they get it.

THE TEN COMMANDMENTS OF BUSINESS
AND HOW TO BREAK THEM

Commandments	*How to Break Them*
Thy Customer is King	If you want the customer to be treated like a king, treat the people you manage like royalty.
Thy Goal Shalt Be to Make a Profit	Focus on the goals and objectives that result in profits.
Rank Hath Its Privileges	Rank has its responsibilities.
Thou Shalt Scorn Nepotism	Make nepotism a state of mind—treat everybody like family.
Thou Shalt Know What Thou Selleth	Marketing is about what people buy, not what you sell.
Thou Shalt Put It in Writing, and Produce It in Triplicate	Talking is three times better than writing in triplicate.
Thou Shalt Covet New Customers	Old customers are more profitable than new customers.
Thou Shalt Have Rules	Corporate culture should replace company rules.
Thou Shalt Not Mix Business and Pleasure	To maximize profits, make business a pleasure
Thou Shalt Labor for Thy Boss	We are all self-employed.

AFTERWORD

I must admit that I approached the task of reviewing this book with some degree of skepticism. After all, I wondered, what could an "advertising guy" out of Kansas City really bring to the cause of advancing the practice of management?

The answer is: a lot!

In *The Ten Commandments of Business—And How to Break Them*, Bill Fromm has put together a complete prescription for improving customer service and, by extension, profitability by focusing on a manager's primary customers: fellow employees. But does the prescription work? My research indicates that it does.

Over the past several years I have been involved in a large-scale research project with my colleague at the Harvard Business School, Jim Heskett. Our findings indicate that companies that have distinguished themselves in the way they hire, train, and treat their employees have experienced:

- Increases in service quality and customer satisfaction of over 50 percent;
- Growth rates 60 to 300 percent greater than competitors;
- Return on sales 200 to 300 percent greater than competitors; and
- Return on assets 150 to 300 percent greater than competitors.

These results stem primarily from improvements in employee retention, which directly impact customer retention. And as chapter seven clearly states: old customers are more profitable than new ones.

In fact, it is a little humbling to discover how much Bill Fromm's "conventional wisdom" converges with my academic findings. At the same time, it is greatly encouraging. And it ought to be encouraging to any manager who reads this book. Because the convergence suggests that if you want to be a great manager, you can make a good start by following the lead of Bill Fromm and taking the advice you had just read in this book.

PROFESSOR LEONARD A. SCHLESINGER
Harvard University Graduate School of Business
November 1990